The Healing Power of Journaling

A Mindful Guide to Self-Reflection, Taming Anxiety, and Learning to Self-Soothe.

Zoe McKey
Communication and Lifestyle Coach

Copyright © 2020 by Zoe McKey. All rights reserved.

No part of this publication may be reproduced, stored in a retrieval system, or transmitted in any form or by any means, electronic, mechanical, photocopying, recording, scanning or otherwise, except as permitted under Section 107 or 108 of the 1976 United States Copyright Act, without the prior written permission of the author.

Limit of Liability/ Disclaimer of Warranty: The author makes no representations or warranties with respect to the accuracy or completeness of the contents of this work and specifically disclaims all warranties, including without limitation warranties of fitness for a particular purpose. No warranty may be created or extended by sales or promotional materials. The advice and recipes contained herein may not be suitable for everyone. This work is sold with the understanding that the author is not engaged in rendering medical, legal or other professional advice or services. If professional assistance is required, the services of a competent professional person should be sought. The author shall not be liable for damages arising herefrom. The fact that an individual, organization of website is referred to in this work as a citation and/or potential source of further information does not mean that the author endorses the information the individual, organization to website may provide or recommendations they/it may make. Further, readers should be aware that Internet websites listed in this work might have changed or disappeared between when this work was written and when it is read.

For general information on the products and services or to obtain technical support, please contact the author.

Table of Contents

Gift Alert 9

Introduction 11

Chapter 1: What Is Anxiety? 25

Chapter 2: False Beliefs That Create Anxiety 53

Chapter 3: Four Steps to Heal Anxiety Wounds 81

Chapter 4: Explore Your Defenses 105

Chapter 5: Abandonment Anxiety 151

Chapter 6: The Art of Self-Soothing 181

Final Words 211

Before You Go… 215

References: 227

Endnotes... 231

Gift Alert

Thank you for choosing my book! I would like to show my appreciation for the trust you gave me by giving a **FREE GIFT** to you!

For more information visit :

www.zoemckey.com

The kit shares *10 key practices to help you to:*

- *discover your true self,*
- *find your life areas that need improvement,*
- *find self-forgiveness,*
- *become better at socializing,*
- *lead a life of gratitude and purpose.*

The kit contains extra actionable worksheets with practice exercises for deeper learning.

Introduction

I remember when my therapist first told me to start journaling to ease my anxieties. It was a lukewarm, humid November evening in Taipei—typhoon season. The relentless wind eerily rattled the old windows of my study. I rolled around in the seventy-year-old bureau chair, holding my head in my hands.

"Is this why I'm paying this therapist? Journaling? Really?"

I felt so disappointed with her advice. If journaling was to be my saving grace, I had better resign myself to the fact that I would never feel less anxious.

Those were difficult days in my life. I had recently discovered that certain aspects of my personality needed improvement. I was snappy, somewhat entitled, and lacking the skills to show my genuine self, which I instead learned to cover with devious defenses. Long story short, I came across some "childhood shit," as Brene Brown would put it, after reading *Adult Children of Emotionally Immature Parents* by Lindsay C. Gibson.

I was very eager to explore deeper, to open up my soul and let the cleansing power of change and healing in. My partner at the time, however, also had a realization triggered by my own. He felt something was not right about me ever since we met, but he couldn't quite put his finger on what. But now that I had figured it out, now he knew it too. And he didn't like it—he didn't like me. He finally admitted that even after spending four years together and some superficial talk of marriage, he never felt fully committed to the idea of spending his life with me. Yet he couldn't accept the idea of not having me, either. He felt wounded by my ignorant behavior in the past and felt unsafe with me.

One day, there was nothing majorly wrong in our relationship—on the surface. Then I read a book and get all excited about self-improvement. The next thing I know, my partner, whom I loved dearly, tells me he has "one leg out of this relationship." What does that mean? Does he need space for a while? Or is he planning to leave me?

I was devastated. Not knowing is one of the most painful and anxiety-provoking conditions you can find yourself in. Maybe I will leave you, maybe not. Maybe you have cancer, maybe not. Maybe you get the scholarship, the promotion, the first "I love you" from your unavailable mother, maybe not. Maybe is a terrible place, in my opinion. Maybe is a castle where anxiety is king.

My partner wrestled with the "should I stay or should I go" question for eight months. And in the end, he decided to leave. Today I know that separating was the best thing we could do for each other and ourselves. We needed wildly different things than what the other could offer. We simply were not a good fit. Yet, at the same time, we were also the perfect match. Nothing about our personality, values, and ways of relating to the world was similar. But we held up the best possible mirror for the other to grow and become a better version of themselves. At least, that's how I feel.

This, of course, is a conclusion I drew in hindsight. Back then, all I wanted was to keep him in my life. I was ready to do anything to make him stay; to accept me, to love me, to see me as "enough."

Have you ever felt the profound terror of potentially losing someone? So deeply that you forgot about your value, pride, and even dignity? I have. I gave up my entire personhood and was committed to make myself into someone who would be "good enough" for him.

By the time you finish this book, you'll see that this kind of problem-solving is not the best path to take. But I didn't know that when my life took this twist. In fact, I didn't know a lot of things. I had no idea what abandonment issues were, why I reacted in certain ways (beyond the conviction "because that's who I am"), or what PTSD or defense mechanisms had to do with my personality. I was unaware and reactive—qualities that understandably pushed my partner away. I was ignorant of my ignorance.

But I was ready to learn. And now I know that I had to lose who I thought I was to find who I really am.

Have you ever experienced such a self-awakening in your life? Has your vague concept of self ever shattered to the ground? Have you ever had to bridge the gap between who you acted like and who you actually were? Were you ever so cornered by frightening circumstances that you chose to outgrow the parts of you that didn't serve you anymore?

If yes, you know that this process doesn't play out without anxiety. When a part of our identity is somehow brought into disrepute—rightfully or not—and we choose to give power and credit to the allegations, we start feeling anxious about who we are as people. Am I a bad person? Did I harm my partner, my children, or people in general? Can I ever change?

Questions such as these are distressing as they are. But now add the potential loss of your significant other into this picture, an unsupportive environment, and utter loneliness, and you'll get overwhelming anxiety.

I don't know what your anxiety story is. Why you feel anxious, what triggers it, when it started, how it manifests. Do you? I didn't know that I could experience anxiety at the level I did in those months. But hey, no one has a condition until they have it. Sometimes it's genetics, sometimes it's early life, sometimes it's just life … but we all experience anxiety at some point.

I was never labeled a chronically anxious person. But after the eight months of "will this guy want me" question mark, I became one. Since then, my life has been dedicated to unlearning how to live with so much anxiety. I am on a good path. I have a partner now who loves me unconditionally and supports me on my journey. I have a fantastic therapist and support group who help me through the difficult moments. And

19

I have a lot of self-awareness and self-worth, which empower me.

I am certainly immensely grateful for everything I have in my life now. But all the things I mentioned are just the positive consequences of one key, crucial habit I developed. And that is journaling.

A journal is a safe space, a discovery board, and a criminal court in one. There you're free to disclose your deepest fears, regrets, obsessions, shames, and desires. You can convict yourself on those pages, admitting that you're guilty as charged of some things you're not proud of. And you can also become a busy lawyer, digging deep into the history of your "crime." What led you to do things you now regret? What made you so "unacceptable"? You'll find plenty of explanation in your upbringing, school years, and later life that justify your "crimes." You can write your most wholehearted acquittal. You can pledge to do differently in the future. Set up an action plan for change.

And you can also vent—about your devastatingly unfulfilling job or your father who is as emotionally available as a lobotomized rock. You can be angry and trash-talk and release all the anxiety and crazy thoughts only a human heart can muster.

Journaling is an amazing outlet. And it's safe. When we're feeling anxious, we crave safety. The good news is, you don't necessarily need anyone to do it. (Although a good therapist's guidance can help.) The bad news is, you need to put in the work. Hours, days, months … years. You need to go down the rabbit hole of your emotions and memories; you need to be brutally honest with yourself.

In this book, I focus on how to journal effectively about your anxiety. How to dig out its origins, clarify your triggers, determine its manifestations, and adopt practices to handle it. But most importantly, I will provide you with a safe space where you can learn to accept and love yourself—anxiety warts and all. This book will explain the whys and hows of anxiety, ask you thought-provoking questions, and provide you with evidence-based techniques that can help you navigate life with more ease while anxious. And yes, ultimately, help loosen the grip anxiety has on you.

You cannot wholly eradicate anxiety from your life. If that's your goal, maybe adjust it to live with anxiety that is well-contained and managed. Besides, anxiety is not all bad. It can be a teacher, an informer, a messenger. If you listen to what it has to say instead of trying to silence it, you might learn something about yourself. You may find an area in your soul that needs attention. You might heal. This is not an overnight journey. Often, this is a journey of a lifetime.

But the pointless days will lead you somewhere. The hours spent journaling. The long talks with your partner. The unsatisfying jobs. Reading romance novels at the beach. The endless browsing through blogs, and books, and Reddit, trying to make sense of who you are, what you believe in, and whether or not it's cool to love fall decorations. These are the things that shape you into who you are.

Disclaimer

Before we get started, I want to tell you, this book in NOT a journal. It is a manual on HOW to journal about your anxiety with purpose and intention. You won't find prompts, cute pictures, and empty pages in here. If that's what you're looking for, my book won't be the right fit for you. This book serves those who already have or are about to have an empty notebook designated for journaling and now want to know the best way to fill it.

Chapter 1: What Is Anxiety?

You are not alone if you know how anxiety feels. It is not picky about who it affects; rich, poor, educated, unschooled, old, young, man, woman, Black, White, dog lover, animal hater. This state of mind crosses all boundaries.

Everybody encounters anxiety a couple times in their life, regardless of how well-established, secure, or mentally stable they are. However, for many of us, anxiety is a recurring or constant visitor. It exists on a spectrum regarding how it affects our life. But what can be done about it?

Anxiety is a classic example of the saying, "What you resist, persists." It is a popular response—especially in Western culture—to repress, ignore, numb, or deny the effect anxious thoughts and emotions have on us. Resorting to any of the practices above will not help us ease our anxiety in the long run. Just like a boomerang, it will come back.

We often fail to consider that anxiety is the messenger of our subconscious mind. If we turn towards it, rather than away from it, we can learn exciting and important things about ourselves. We can step on the path of genuine healing. To use the message of anxiety to our benefit, we need to break up with the idea that anxiety is a sign of weakness, a shameful part of our being. We need to adopt an attitude of curiosity, one that accepts our fears as a part of our gentle, sentient heart, continually seeking growth and healing.

When we approach anxiety as a teacher, we can learn valuable lessons about our needs. Our innermost self is trying to tell us to pay attention to an area ready to grow.

We can experience anxiety in many forms—obsessions, intrusive thoughts, insomnia, and excessive worrying, just to name a few. If we choose to respond to these symptoms with denial or repression led by shame, we will not rid ourselves of them. They will secretly team up against us in a particular place of our psyche. Intrusive thoughts like "you'll never be enough," "you're broken," "you messed it up last time, and you're going to mess it up again," "after such a long time of abstinence you did it again, there's no going back now," and "you just ruined everything" will flood our mind.

Let's look at the two ways we can react. If we respond to these thoughts from a place of shame, we'll feel small and powerless. We'll be prompted to live up to the message of our brain to avoid cognitive dissonance. So, often, we'll actually say or do something to "destroy everything." It is our hardwired response.

However, suppose we can recognize anxiety for what it is, just an emotion, and take a look at its message from a place of curiosity. In that case, we can discover a vital area we need to improve in our life. Let's take the thought, "You messed it up last time, and you're going to mess it up again." From a learning point of view, we can zoom in on the failure we're so afraid of repeating. We can open up our journal and answer the following questions:

What led to that failure? What were the consequences of that failure? What have you learned since then? Why are you so sure you'll do it again? If you happen to fail, what's the worst that can happen? And then what? And then what?

....
....
....
....
....
....
....
....

Answering these questions, we can zoom in on the core problem. Say we conclude we lack self-confidence and that we tend to expect the worst. Good. Now, what can we do to change that?

……………………………………………
…………
……………………………………………
…………
……………………………………………
…………

Anxiety can direct you towards healing, my dear reader, if you listen to its messages. It can help you embrace who you are and guide you towards who you want to become. Maybe people labeled you in the past. They told you that you are too much. Or the opposite, that you are not challenging enough and they can't promise a relationship or friendship with you. You may have concluded that you are broken in some way, inadequate, and you then gave up on yourself. Or the contrary, the criticism fired you up, and you decided to change yourself. To shapeshift … for them.

But you must start letting go of these beliefs. Hopefully, as you read through this book, you'll realize that there's absolutely nothing wrong with you. You are not broken. You are not too much. You are challenging enough. You can shine a light on people's lives. But what you need the most now is to embrace, very tightly, those wounded parts of yourself. Keep them close, soothe them like you would a sick child. Those parts of you don't need repair. They need healing.

The answers to tend to your anxiety-ridden parts are not "out there." They are in you. You want your peace of mind. With the help of this guided journal, we will find your innermost answers and solutions. The best part of anxiety is that it provides helpful clues on what areas need attention and which parts of your soul were injured and need healing.

What Is Anxiety?

Evolutionarily, anxiety served a purpose to ensure our survival. A little sizzle in a bush here, a faint growl there, and our body became hyper-alert to danger, releasing adrenaline to supplement our fight-or-flight response. But today, we don't face the same triggers as we did thousands of years ago. Our response to danger, however, has not evolved as fast as our environment. We give the same reaction to triggers like a phone ringing or seeing a change in our spouse's smile as we did in prehistoric times. Needless to say, the dangers we face today are less lethal in most cases, yet we meet them with the same life-or-death attitude.

Have you ever lost sleep over your financial future even though you were financially stable? Have you ever worried excessively about the health of your children? Have you felt antsy to leave your relationship, even though your partner was loving and you were happy? Can you sit still and spend a day doing "nothing"? Or do you ruminate about the many things you could do to make something of your life? Have you ever feared having a fatal illness? Have you ever asked, "Am I safe?"

These are just some examples of how anxiety manifests in our brains. We know how these thoughts make us feel awfully well. But could you describe what anxiety is? It is crucial to name it and pin down the emotion to know what exactly we are dealing with. Knowing when we feel anxious and being able to affirm, "I feel anxiety," is already a soothing experience. We are not crazy; we are not about to have a heart attack. It's just anxiety.

Psychologist Sheryl Paul defined anxiety as follows:

"Anxiety is a feeling of dread, agitation, or foreboding associated with a danger that does not exist in the present moment. It can also be defined as a general and pervasive sense of dis-ease without an identified source. Anxiety, while often experienced in the body, is a head state that keeps its prisoners trapped in the realm of unproductive and fear-based thinking. Anxiety keeps you on high alert, and at its core, lives the belief that you're not okay, that you'll never be okay, and that you're not safe physically, emotionally, and/or spiritually. Anxiety and trust are mutually exclusive."[i]

Thoughts, compulsive actions, and physical sensations are symptoms of anxiety. When you feel like you can't eat, that you're going to throw up since you're so agitated, these can be anxiety's physical manifestations. Finding a knot in your neck and immediately jumping on the internet to research what it could be, that's a compulsive action triggered by anxious thoughts. What makes matters worse is the interpretation we attach to our anxious observations, such as "the knot must mean I have cancer."

It's essential to separate the symptoms and the meaning that we attach to them. We need to get as intimate and familiar with our anxiety symptoms and name them before sticking any substance to them. In the example of the knot on your neck, you can observe to yourself, "I feel anxiety because I noticed this bump on my neck. This is something I've felt in the past, too. They come and go. Whenever I notice a knot, I have the tendency to jump to the conclusion that I have cancer, but that's actually very unlikely. I have no proof of that, and I don't want to harm myself with needless worrying."

To help you notice, recognize, and effectively journal about your anxiety symptoms, I wrote a list of how anxiety can manifest in your body.

As we discussed, we can group these symptoms into three categories:

Thoughts:

- What if I'm dying?
- What if I never discover what I'm born for?
- What if I make a mistake marrying X?
- What if I don't actually want children, and I'll be a terrible parent?
- What if my business collapses?
- What if the stocks I invested in fall?

Physical Symptoms:

- Tight stomach
- Chest pain or tightness
- Difficulty taking a deep breath
- Shallow breath
- Hyperventilating
- Insomnia
- Chronic fatigue

- Restlessness, difficulty being still
- Headaches
- Sweating
- Feeling of dis-ease
- Lightheadedness
- "Empty brain" feeling

Behavioral Symptoms/Compulsions:

- Perfectionism
- Irritability
- Anger
- Compulsive talking or complete silence
- Addictions
- Compulsive attempts to seek reassurance[ii]

This list is not exhaustive by any means. Still, it can give you a good idea about what a colorful palette of manifestation anxiety has.

Think about how anxiety manifests in your body, mind, and behavior.

When I'm anxious, I often have the following thoughts:
……………………………………………………………
……………………………………………………………
……………………………………………………………
……………………………………………………………

When I'm anxious, I often have these physical symptoms:
……………………………………………………………

....
....
....
....
....
....

When I'm anxious, I often behave this way:

....
....
....
....
....
....
....
....

Write about how you experience anxiety in as much detail as you can.

In the physical realm, anxiety can flood your body with adrenaline, giving you the sensation that you're in constant danger. In more mild cases, anxiety manifests in headaches, muscle pain or tension, the struggle of taking a deep breath, or difficulty sleeping. In the mental realm, we get trapped with certain thoughts, ruminating day and night trying to find an answer to create certainty and safety. In chronic cases, anxiety can lead us to shut down our emotions altogether, causing a state of numbness. All of the sensations described above are unpleasant. We want to live free from their grip.

Where Is Our Anxiety Coming From?

The roots of our anxiety can be traced back to our early life. Our upbringing, the relationship with our parents, our experience at school, and adults' behavior around us could all be responsible for our anxiety triggers today.

Why is it important to learn about and understand the origin story of our anxiety? Because this understanding helps us normalize our behavior. In the context of our past, our reaction to certain stimuli is not abnormal. Quite the contrary, it makes a lot of sense. Looking at our anxiety—and ourselves—through this lens, we can release some of the shame we feel.

Predisposition to anxiety can also be inherited. If one or both of one's parents had anxiety issues, they are more likely to have it themselves. Children can easily absorb the dysfunctional anxiety-management patterns of their parents. That's how they think anxiety should be handled, or, simply, they won't know any other way to deal with this debilitating state of mind. For better or worse, they will repeat the pattern they learned. Even if, deep down, they know their behavior will not have the outcome they wish.

Did you recognize yourself in the paragraph above? Do you think you're responding to anxiety just like your parents did? For example, when you're ruminating after an anxious outbreak (because, oh yes, we do ruminate after one of those), do you scold yourself for behaving just like your mother did? Do you see your reactions as being your caregivers'?

If yes, that's okay. Suppose you never unlearned your childhood conditioning, and you never replaced the unhelpful reactions with helpful ones. In that case, it's absolutely normal that you'd seek soothing any way you can.

The good news is you are not doomed to repeat all the mistakes of your parents. You can change even the profoundly rooted behaviors with patience and practice. I know this is hard to believe, because one of the anxious mind's main slogans is "I will never change." The always-never dichotomy is a typical attributive of anxiety; fatalistic, all-or-nothing thinking is partially the cause of our distress.

In this book, we'll learn to question, dissect, and deconstruct these thoughts. We will change the language you use internally by changing the beliefs you have about yourself. And no, it's not me who will do it. I'm not trying to sell you snake oil; I will not tell you what to think. It's you who will reach the conclusion that you're able to change; that you're able to turn around your life and harness your true potential.

Think about your main caregivers. How would you describe their anxiety management? What triggered your parents' anxiety? How did their anxiety affect you?

……………………………………………………
……………
……………………………………………………
……………
……………………………………………………
……………
……………………………………………………
……………

Anxiety Is a Defense Mechanism

In some sense, anxiety is meant to protect us from the pain of experiencing intense emotions we never learned to manage. Optimally, as we grow up, our parents teach us the tools and rituals to navigate difficult emotions through good examples and in-depth conversations. If, as children, we didn't learn how to handle anger, fear, distrust, jealousy, sadness, frustration, or loneliness, we have no clue how to tend to them. This is when anxiety steps in as a decoy to protect us from the more significant pain we would be feeling. It moves our attention from the realm of the heart to the safer space of the mind. The mind starts to ruminate, distract, and deny, instead of allowing us to feel our pain and soothe it with care and attention.

When you look at your anxiety from this angle, is it surprising that it exists? How do you tend to your anger? Or your loneliness? Do you tend to think of the following thoughts? You're quick to blame the person who made you angry. You rationalize that you don't like people in general; you choose not to mingle with them, and you're not lonely at all. These responses are all the confabulations of the mind. They help us be less unhappy in the short term, but our problems will not solve themselves. I will dedicate an entire chapter to defense mechanisms later in this book.

Other Sources of Anxiety

Our early school experience is fertile soil for learning to be anxious. Peer pressure and our desperate need to fit in, to be accepted by our classmates, and to meet specific education standards are things that can lead to developing anxiety. Scientific papers proved that about 20 percent of children have different learning styles than what schools provide. Imagine being an introvert, yet being forced to speak up in front of a loud classroom, or having the need to move while learning but being bullied—or shamed—into sitting still. Often, kids who don't fit the box of conventional education are labeled "misbehaving," "troubled," or "good-for-nothings." They are often publicly humiliated. They become the classroom highlight for being an excellent example of what a lousy child looks like or a cautionary tale of how not to be. These experiences leave scars.

Would you say you experienced anxiety in your school years? If yes, what triggered it? What belief systems did you have about yourself as a child that made you feel anxious?

....
....

....
....
....
....
....
....

Modern media is another anxiety booster. Commercials and advertisements deliberately target our inadequacy. "You're not thin enough." "You're not traveled enough." "You're not rich enough." The bottom line is, you are not enough. The my-life-is-better-than-yours social media culture just adds a layer of distress to our struggles. Before, we only saw superstars as the ideals we should follow. Now we can see that even Sally from grade school made it while we toss papers around in the accounting cubicle of a carwash. Some stories on social media can dishearten even the most confident. Still, it has a much larger impact on those predisposed to anxiety. The pressure to keep up with everyone's stupendous life and the angst to be validated (through likes and other forms of peer engagement) can push people to the limit of their wits.

Conventional news media also doesn't help. All the catastrophes, deaths, shootings, killings, and earthquakes are broadcast in a tight chain one after the other. If we are avid news consumers, it's not hard to believe that our world is a dangerous place, that people have to be kept at arm's length, and that everything foreign is a hazard. I don't find it surprising at all that some people set up their home as a military base in case the apocalypse hits us in the next month or so.

Do you think media outlets make you more anxious? If yes, what messages are the most triggering to you?

....
....
....
....
....
....
....
....

When we're young, the world suggests that we grow up, man up, woman up, and act like an adult. When we're adults, we get the message that we should do everything in our power to keep our youthful looks and spirit. In either case, the takeaway is that we're not acceptable the way we are. Is it really abnormal that we feel all that anxiety?

Chapter 2: False Beliefs That Create Anxiety

"What? You think your way of thinking is normal? It's not normal!" said my ex in a heated argument. I can't recall what we were talking about, but his comeback had to do with either my beliefs or my way of handling conflict.

Being labeled "not normal" is shame-provoking; especially if it comes from someone important to us. Have you ever been labeled as abnormal, crazy, overreacting, overly emotional, impossible, or weird? How did it feel?

……………………………………………………………

....

....

....

....

....

....

Only a few of us can genuinely brush off labels such as the ones above. Those who have strong self-confidence and rarely feel anxious are probably not reading this book. The rest of us, who get flooded by shame and a deep sense of inadequacy, spiral into anxious thoughts about our worth when hearing these judgments (because that's what they are). Even more than that, we tend to embrace the negative statements and incorporate them into our self-image, our identity.

I am Zoe, the inadequate one, who is too stupid to make sense, to react how she's supposed to, and to behave like a normal human being.

I walked around with this "mantra" for a couple years. I didn't understand why, but I always felt so very anxious when I spent time with my ex. When he asked me something, my voice would chuckle, and I'd say something unnatural, in an odd tone, squeezing one of my hands with the other to muster the courage to even talk. I was so terrified that I'd say something wrong. Often, he'd just look at me with a gaze, which shouted how displeased he was with my reply. Sometimes he'd ask me "Why do you talk weirdly?" or "Why do you smile when you're talking about a sad thing such as this? Have you ever considered how abnormal that is?"

And bum, there it was ... my life-and-death effort to be "normal" was classified abnormal again. Encounters like this only enforced my belief that there was something fundamentally wrong with me. I became even more anxious when I opened my mouth the next time, which only prompted my ex to call me the things I feared even more often. Can you see the vicious, reinforcing loop here?

How did I break out of it? I didn't. We broke up. And just like that, from one day to the next, he was out of my life. But his words didn't leave. They lingered. They echoed in my head, reflecting back in my work, in my relationships, in the stories I told myself.

When we experience painful events, we create an emotional response (it often has to do with anxiety). Then we fabricate a story to explain this event to ease our pain. In my case, I told myself that I needed to improve and grow for the wrong reasons—that my ex was right about me, and that I was fortunate to have him point out how deeply flawed I was. In other words, I turned against myself. It was the only way I could rationalize the pain I felt in that relationship. It was the only way I could stay.

Have you ever explained your pain with a creative story? Have you ever stayed in a toxic work environment thinking "this is just how work is"? Or, "Nowhere will I be paid just as good as here"? Have you ever excused your mother's controlling behavior, saying "this is how she was raised" or "after all the hardships she's been through …"? If yes, write about it here:

....
....
....
....
....
....
....
....

The problem with these stories is that they become our identity, belief system, and knee-jerk reactions. And we organize our life around these false beliefs, creating situations that will confirm our thoughts. For example, I bought into the idea that I was not good enough, my reactions were not normal, and voila, I started acting the way I believed I was.

What are your false core beliefs that provoke anxiety?

It's time to take out your journal to answer the following questions. Please take some time to think about what kind of self-talk you have. How do you describe yourself in times of distress? What do you tell yourself when you fail?

1. ………………

2. ………………

3. ………………

(For example, "I believe I will never be a good enough partner because my behavior is abnormal.")

You can write more than three examples.

Next, take a look at the examples you just wrote down. How do they make you feel right now? How do they make you feel when you're in a situation that prompts them? Write about these sensations in as much detail as you can. What kind of physical manifestations follow these thoughts? What action do you take after the false beliefs pop up?

1. ....

2. ....

3. ....

(For example, right now, thinking about not being enough and being abnormal makes me feel slightly nauseated. It hurts me so much that there was a time in my life when I whipped my soul a thousand times a day to change for someone who was never going to accept me. Back in the day, I felt like a worthless failure because of this belief. I felt like I was swimming against the current; I tried to improve, but I knew I couldn't, as I knew I was abnormal and beyond help.)

Who or what "sold" you this false belief? Try to recall when you encountered the false belief first. While we tend to stumble onto people who make us feel a certain way in our adult life, quite often, the "original perpetrator" comes from our childhood.

1. ………………

2. ………………

3. ………………

(For example, my recent ex was the one who leveled up my sense of inadequacy. But the first people who made me feel awfully abnormal were my paternal grandparents.)

It can be a challenge to admit to ourselves that we believe we are imperfect in some way because of someone else's opinion. Yet, it is a significant step. In this way, we can detach from the false belief. It is not a verdict, it is not our fundamental self, and it is just a painful input in our heart.

Go back to the first list of the exercise above and rewrite your examples the following way:

"I learned to believe I will never be good enough and that I have abnormal behavior from my paternal grandparents."

1.   ……………….

2. ………………

3. ………………

Attribute each of the painful stories to their original creator. It was never you.

Now it's time to rewrite these beliefs. Write an honest assessment of yourself in the context of the false belief. Don't just write "I'm normal" if you originally wrote "I'm abnormal." This kind of "fake it till you make it" won't help. Instead, write an accurate description of how you think you show up in the world. You can even admit that you genuinely believe in the false belief at this moment. But try to recall at least three events from the near past when the mistaken belief was wildly contradicted.

1. ....

2. ....

3. ....

(For example, I still believe that I am not good enough sometimes. At the same time, I made amazing friends in the past six months who are actively seeking my friendship and my advice, confirming that I am smart and articulate. I have a loving boyfriend who tells me how much he loves and appreciates me every day. I received two emails last month from readers who told me how much my books helped them.)

Get as detailed as you want with your rewriting. Once you're done, read your words out loud. Think about the lovely memories that contradict your painful, false beliefs. What if you re-read these lines every day? What if you believed them to be true? What if they could shape your life going forward? What if you were normal? What if your insecurity born from judgmental words was accepted to be a natural reaction? What if, in fact, you were interesting, and a great friend, and a loving partner, and good at what you do? What if you told yourself these stories?

One of the things you need to do going forward is totally accepting the reality of who and how you are. You came into this world being a unique person with extraordinary things to offer to the world. So that's you, the real you. There's nothing wrong with who and how you are.

The challenge in life is learning how to discover and manage your authentic self; the desires, goals, and needs of this authentic self. You need to work through this challenge to start getting your needs met. While being respectful of other people's needs and goals for themselves, you need to learn to not allow others to disrespect and discourage your authentic self. To do this, you need to peel off many layers of false beliefs and be secure about who you are and what you need.

The work of discovering my authentic self has already taken me two years, and I'm still learning. It's a long process, so I won't even try to bamboozle you with a promise that you'll find yourself by completing one exercise. Or by reading this book. But reading this book and completing the practices here will get you closer to knowing your authentic self.

Self-discovery is time-consuming because you have to approach it as a scientist might. You observe your behavior and take note (at least mentally, but preferably physically) of it. Did you behave according to your beliefs? Yes or no? If not, how was your behavior different? How often do you act contrary to your thoughts? If you make moves contrary to your beliefs frequently, isn't this a perfect time to question your beliefs?

For example, you believe you are outdoorsy. Still, every time your friends plan an outdoor adventure, you either bail at the last minute or participate but not enjoy it at all. Are you genuinely outdoorsy, then, or do you just like watching nature documentaries? The two things are not the same. You can note this observation and learn to accept that you are not really a nature adventurer. Seek activities that bring more joy to your authentic self. You can organize a TV dinner with your friends where you watch nature documentaries. You'll enjoy yourself much more, and your friends might get inspired to check out a new outdoor adventure based on what they saw at dinner.

Think about distressing free-time activities you engage in. Why do you do them? What's your reasoning? What stories do you tell yourself about the activity? How do you feel before, during, and after doing this activity?

....
....
....

....
....

My example here would be heavy weight-lifting. While I generally like going to the gym and pushing my limits, there was a time in my life when I allowed myself to be bullied into doing more than what laid in my optimal comfort zone. Usually I felt longing and excitement before going to the gym, pumped up and entertained while there, and satisfied and energized after. But when I started lifting uncomfortably heavy weights, I noticed a shift in my mood. I procrastinated in anxiety before hitting my otherwise safe space, I felt scared during, and relieved after. None of these states of mind were ideal. Why did I do it? Because I wanted to please my partner at the time. I told myself the story that if I became strong enough in his eyes, he would love me more.

Ever since I had this realization, I gradually tuned down on heavy weight-lifting and I went back to the activities that challenged me but also filled my heart—and muscles—with joy.

Another question to ask while you do your scientific self-analysis is, "Did I behave in compliance with my emotional needs? Did I act according to my best self's expectations?" Use the example you wrote about above and answer these questions in the context of that story. Explore why you behaved the way you did.

…………………………………………….
…………………………………………….
…………………………………………….
…………………………………………….

To complete this exercise, think about precisely how you want to be when you feel yourself drifting into doing something that makes you anxious. Come up with boundary-asserting sentences you can use when someone tries to pressure you into something unappealing to you or you are bullying yourself into an activity to please someone.

………………………………………………
………………………………………………
………………………………………………
……………………………………………

You need to have a gold standard in front of you to be able to measure deviation—"this is how I want to behave" vs. "this is how I actually behaved." How can you fill in the gap? How can you do better?

……………………………………………

This is what "knowing thyself" actually means. Knowing exactly what you like, what you would like, and what you need. If you know all that, it is not that hard to notice things you don't like, wouldn't like, and don't need.

I know that breaking free from being, doing, and saying things to please others is scary. If you tend to assume that you're somehow flawed or unworthy based on someone's opinion, you really want to apply the art of self-inquiry. Sit down and ask yourself hard questions, answer them from a place of genuine, deep self-knowledge, and compare your answer to what the other person tells you. If someone tells you that you are weak for not loving nature adventures, or lifting heavy weights, ask yourself, "Am I really weak because of this? Is this true? Do I consider this a weakness? Do these activities hold and meaning or value to me, or am I obsessing about them to please X? Would I do them if X wasn't be in the picture?"

Ask similar questions to yourself to dig to the bottom of your truth. You can also explore contradictory evidence. For example, if someone called you weak, find areas of your life where you feel you're strong. What are you strong at? Maybe you're not a weightlifter, but you already ran two marathons. Or you can work on your projects, finish them before their deadlines, and produce outstanding work quality. That's strength. Find your truth. Find what matters to you, what you believe in.

You may have been quick to make assessments and arrive at conclusions about your acceptability and worthiness in the past. Still, now it's time to approach this a different way. The jumping to conclusions has to go on pause. Jumping to conclusions, in a sense, means adopting false beliefs based on someone's opinion. This is considered a "distortion of reality," and distortions of reality can cause tremendous anxiety.

The truth can cause anxiety too. But it's the truth that we want to be operating from, not the perceived truth or the distorted truth—the authentic self's actual reality. You could discover something about your authentic self that you want to change—for your own benefit, not to please others. You might realize you were not behaving according to how you'd like to. Your actions don't satisfy your emotional need to feel balanced and in tune with yourself. This realization can trigger some anxiety in you. You may worry about how long the disliked behavior has been going on, who you've hurt in the process, if you'll be able to change it …

You need to be sure that you are loved and accepted by yourself despite your shortcomings. Commit to the feeling of self-love. You deserve that. And you owe it to yourself. You can't merely rely only on other people to reassure your worth. You need to do it first. It's up to you to ask yourself: am I enough for me? If the answer is no, you also owe it to yourself to examine why you feel that way. Is it really because of how you are? Or is someone implying that you're not enough? If, deep down, you disagree with the implication, release the situation (or person), and go forward to create a better position where your genuine self has a chance of being accepted.

Read the last paragraph again. What thoughts popped up in your head? Explore the questions above, think about them, and answer them. Create a blueprint for self-love and self-acceptance.

....
....
....
....
....
....
....
....

What to Do When You Feel Deep Down That You Don't Meet Your Own Needs

If you feel that you are "not enough" because you want to do better, commit to a plan that will guide you to the desired behavior. Meeting your own expectations, your authentic self's emotional needs, is your job as an adult. It was your parents' job to help you with that when you were a kid, but now it's your job. If your parents didn't do well with that, two things happen: (1) you don't really know how to look out for your own emotional needs, and (2) you feel angry about having to take care of your emotional needs now. No one did it for you when they were supposed to, and dammit, someone ought have!

So first, acknowledge and know your needs. Second, assess your situation. Are your needs being met? Are they able to get met? If yes, that's great …

If no, you can get mad and frustrated at the world, but that is a helpless victim's stance that will not bring you closer to happiness. In fact, it will do the opposite.

If you assess that your needs are not being met, it's up to you to make the shifts in your life. That can mean so many things, and we will talk about that later in the book. We'll work on the art of self-inquiry. This has a lot to do with speaking from the heart and not using close-ended statements such as, "I am a terrible communicator and cannot change."

With our tendencies and early life programming, we will always be susceptible to false beliefs. But we have to keep in mind that it's up to us to sift and sort through our views until we land on something that feels right for us.

So let's do this final self-assessment in this chapter:

What are my main needs?

……………………………………………
……………………………………………
……………………………………………
……………………………………………

Are they being met?

……………………………………………
……………………………………………

If not, how can I help myself to meet my needs? What can I do? Should I ask for help? Who should I ask—a friend, a therapist?

……………………………………………
……………………………………………

Chapter 3: Four Steps to Heal Anxiety Wounds

In her book, *The Wisdom of Anxiety*, Sheryl Paul talks about four steps we need to explore to mitigate the effects anxiety has on us. These steps are curiosity, compassion, stillness, and gratitude. Based on personal experience, I can attest that her description is accurate. Let's cruise through her points together.

1. Curiosity

Successful anxiety management stems in shifting from repression to genuine curiosity of our inner world. There's no magic wand that will make this shift happen in one second. It's a commitment where we frequently remind ourselves that we intend to be curious.

A quick tip here: On my journey of self-discovery, I noticed that I am slow to learn and fast to forget. Therefore, I wrote the best ideas and most important habits I want to adopt on a Post-it. I stuck these notes on my wall somewhere visible to review them as many times as possible. I have one by my dining table, one on my desk, and one on the fridge door. Some of these notes are active reminders to keep an open, curious mind instead of a judgmental one.

My goal is to read the notes repeatedly to carve them into my conscious memory and make them immediately accessible.

Back to curiosity, I have a little journaling exercise for you. Take a few minutes to write down what anxiety feels like to you. Remember to approach anxiety with friendliness. It is not the enemy but the messenger. We don't shoot the messenger. Noticing when anxiety appears and naming how it manifests in you are crucial first steps in breaking free. Answer the following questions:

Where do I feel anxiety in my body?
……………………………………………………
……………
……………………………………………………
……………

What thoughts do I have when I feel anxious? Are they repetitive?
……………………………………………………
……………

....
....

When did I first have this thought? When did I start feeling anxious about X?

....
....
....
....

How did my caretakers handle anxiety?

....
....
....
....

How did my caretakers handle MY anxiety?

....
....
....
....

Every time an anxiety symptom pops up, note to yourself something like "anxiety, in the form of intrusive thoughts" or "anxiety, in the form of shallow breathing." If you can, write down each time you feel anxiety, what triggered it, and what the symptom is. Act like a curious scientist who is collecting data for a research project. You are the subject of this project. As you may know, the more relevant data a study has, the better conclusions the scientist will draw. This is essential in finding the best solutions to a triggering situation.

A great way to deal with anxiety is through individual self-help work, whether it be one-on-one with a therapist or another kind of introspective process. When it comes to working on this challenge, we need to uncover ways to engage with ourselves, leading to healthy, satisfying self-talk. And that's no easy task when emotions are being triggered.

But let's see if we can take that challenge head-on. The challenge would be to transition from being one who reacts to things that trigger anxiety to one who *talks about* being triggered. That is the next step, talking about it, rather than being it or doing it.

How could you remind yourself that your anxiety is just a messenger? How would you soothe yourself? What would you tell yourself to avoid spiraling into the habitual response?

....
....
....

……………………………………………

Step two is: how will you receive it? If you remind yourself that you feel triggered, would that alleviate your anxiety and refocus your attention? Or would that make you more triggered? Maybe it would make you step back and take a breath and ease up on the escalation of negative emotions.

……………………………………………
……………………………………………
……………………………………………
……………………………………………

We'll better address the de-escalation process once the first part takes place successfully: the part of saying that you're feeling triggered (in a calm way) rather than acting triggered.

So, the challenge at this point is, can you stop your triggered state of mind in its tracks? Can you see yourself feeling triggered as you are actually feeling triggered by someone else? And can you put the sensation of feeling triggered and anxious into words of honest, authentic self-expression?

It would be great to uncover some more information about what your anxiety triggers are. Do you have a sense of what is happening in you when you are feeling triggered? When you react as less than your best self, when you feel pinched off and shut down, emotionally, when you are feeling distant, small, wounded, or resentful, what is going on inside? Do you have any words to convey what the feelings are?

....
....
....
....
....
....
....
....
....
....
....
....

It's okay if you can't de-escalate your anxiety the first time you try to nip the trigger in the bud. Take a note of what you told yourself. Did it work? How did it make you feel? If you were successful, keep exploring the same ideas and words you used. If you weren't, try to come up with another approach for the next time.

This exploration of feeling emotionally triggered and anxious, and managing past pain in the present, is a heavy topic. It is loaded with all kinds of emotion. And I commend you for taking on such a journey, because it's worth it. These triggers will go with you everywhere; after all, they're yours, so it's wise to know everything you can about them and come to terms with them.

2. Compassion

The second step to healing is meeting your anxiety with compassion and care. How often have you heard "get over it," "you're too sensitive," "you're a baby," "stop whining and behave like normal people do"?

Do you tell yourself the same sentences?

No wonder your heart is heavy. It's time to release these thoughts and learn to meet your anxiety with acceptance. I know this is not an easy task, given that your needs as a child were probably met with silencing, being ignored, or being shamed.

We are going to learn how to rewire our brain; slowly but surely. The key concept we need to address is the notion of finding and having compassion for your soft spot. A place where you need to be handled with gentleness, regardless of how much sense your sensitivity may or may not make. Once you uncover the anxiety-related pain-points or sensitivities left over from your childhood, you have the choice to be supportive and compassionate, leading to a healthy relationship with yourself. Or be dismissive and shaming, leading to a toxic relationship.

Why is self-compassion important? Because when we are working within the framework of a restoration of the true self, having compassion for our wounded self is vital. It's safe to say that these issues (your soft spots) are disturbing and anxiety-provoking when you do not accept them. Emotionally-triggering problems that are not healed are exposed to the world that keeps poking at them. It's a formula for a stressful life. But when you can see clearly where your pain points are, when you can choose to say, "I accept myself and will approach this problem with understanding and caring," you make a point of protecting the emotional bruises. You don't want to live like a Pavlovian dog, like a puppet on a string. You want to be free, and you want to be able to separate the pain of the past from what's happening in the present. Practice to hold space for your pain compassionately.

As a consequence, feelings of self-love and self-trust emerge. Which lead to fulfillment—both emotional and spiritual.

Are you able to wrap your mind around the notion of proper self-care and real personal responsibility for your life? Can you say, "This is what I want for my life. This is what I don't want for my life. Living at the mercy of my anxiety is definitely not something I want"?

Exercise:

Have you heard the word tonglen? It is a Buddhist practice I learned in Pema Chödrön's book, *When Things Fall Apart*. This practice helps us reverse the habit of pushing away unwanted feelings. It works like this: you breathe in what you feel is unwanted and breathe out what is wanted.

You take in pain and send out spaciousness and relief, as Chödrön puts it. Tonglen is not how we usually respond to unwanted feelings, right? We usually push them away instead of letting them in. When we practice tonglen, we rewire our minds to accept our pain and fear. We become more acquainted with these rejected parts of ours; we offer them space, accept them, and gently release them.

Tonglen also reminds us that many other people share our pain. If you have the capacity, you can breathe in their sorrow as well and release relief. This is a beautiful practice to acknowledge how interconnected we all are and recognize our shared humanity.[iii]

3. Stillness

The third step to heal anxiety is to allow ourselves to slow down and be still. Have you ever noticed that the quicker you move, the less attention you can pay to your surroundings? If you walk slowly enough, you may even be able to read a book. If you're sprinting, all your focus is on keeping up the speed and not falling on your nose. The takeaway is this, the more we slow down, the more we can grasp from our outer—and inner—world.

Anxiety can actually be looked at as a built-in alarm system telling us, "Slow down, you don't give me enough attention." You don't need to carve out hours from your day to practice stillness. Sometimes a few moments of re-centering can help.

In 2019 I went to a one-week meditation retreat in Plum Village, France. The monastery had an excellent daily practice there involving the large bell in the yard. At random times a nun would stop by the bell and ring it. Once we heard the sound of the bell, we stopped whatever we were doing and opened our senses to the sound. As long as the bell's sound lingered, we focused inward. We got in touch with our hearing, our breath. It was a couple second of stillness, a reminder to be mindful of the present moment. Once the bell's resonance was gone, we resumed doing whatever we were doing before the sound.

I loved this mini habit, so I decided to continue it after my meditation camp was over. I downloaded an app on my phone called Mindful Bell. This app releases bell sounds at random times, just like the nuns did at the camp. Whenever I hear the bell, I stop to re-center myself; I remind myself that life happens here, now, in the present moment.

It could be helpful to introduce a similar habit to your life. We do a much better job at managing our anxiety when we put in the practice we need when we're in a neutral state of mind. If we order our fire extinguisher on Amazon when our house is already on fire … well, you can imagine how that will go.

Practice stillness. Stop to notice your breaths. Focus on one of your senses at a time. What can you see now? What can you hear now? Smell? Taste? Touch?

Journaling exercise:

Meditate over the following questions. They are designed to help you slow down. Ask yourself from a position of curiosity:

What happens when I take the time to meditate?

....
....
....
....

What would happen if I just immerse myself in the beautiful landscape I see instead of taking a photo to post it?

....
....
....
....

What would happen if I snuggled with my partner or think about three things I'm grateful for when I wake up instead of reaching for my phone?

…………………………………………………
……………
…………………………………………………
……………

What would happen if, before sleep, I read inspiring quotes instead of scrolling the news?

…………………………………………………
……………
…………………………………………………
……………

What would happen if I meet the parts of myself I've deemed unlovable with gentleness and care? Inviting them in, taking a look at them, and compassionately breathing in their pain?

……………………………………………
……………
……………………………………………
……………

4. Gratitude

The fourth step that helps us overcome anxiety is gratitude. Allow yourself to be grateful not only for your blessings but also for your challenges. Be thankful for the gift of anxiety, which, if you pay attention to, can lead you to immense growth. It's difficult to imagine being grateful for anxiety, but if you try doing it anyway, you'll see it makes sense. Inviting your concerns into your heart with acceptance can bring you into your innermost home. I encourage you to take the hand of your anxiety and explore it. You never know what gems you'll find in the depth of it. I don't know either; it's a unique experience for all of us.

Allow yourself to discover that you're good and enough. You can take care of yourself. There is beauty and strength inside you. Allow your grip to loosen and your awareness to deepen, and finally see yourself as you really are. You are lucky and blessed. To be alive. To be as self-aware as you are. Not many people acknowledge that unmanaged anxiety keeps them from the life they deserve to live. Even fewer people take steps to change that situation. But you did. You admitted some difficult things to yourself. You bought this book. You have a lot to be grateful for. One is your strong spirit.

Three things I am grateful for in general:

……………………………………………………
……………
……………………………………………………
……………
……………………………………………………
……………

Three things I am grateful for learning thanks to anxiety:

……………………………………………………
……………
……………………………………………………
……………
……………………………………………………
……………

Three things I am grateful for healing in myself:

Chapter 4: Explore Your Defenses

Let's talk a little bit about Sigmund Freud …

I'd like to have a discussion with you about the subject of defense mechanisms. This term was often used by Sigmund Freud in his psychoanalytic theory. According to Freud, a defense mechanism is a technique used by the ego to protect against anxiety. Defense mechanisms are created to protect the mind against feelings and thoughts too difficult for the conscious mind to cope with. Sometimes, defense mechanisms can keep unwanted or shame-triggering thoughts and impulses from entering the conscious mind.[iv]

In his personality model, Freud distinguishes three parts: the ego, the superego, and the id. The ego is the reality-checker part of one's personality. The superego pushes the ego to behave in a moral and idealistic way. On the other hand, the id works to fulfill all wants, needs, and impulses—whatever those may be. The id and superego are often in conflict; what we want is not always the right thing to do. So the ego gets signals in the form of anxiety that whispers, "Things are not going the way they should." The ego, wanting to solve the discomfort, reacts by employing some defense mechanism to diminish anxiety's unpleasant feelings. In Freud's belief, defense mechanisms protect the ego from the id's conflicts with the superego and reduce anxiety.

Everybody uses defense mechanisms to protect themselves from emotional pain: something to put a wall up between the outside world (including other people) and their true and honest feelings.

Being stoic and emotionless is a defense mechanism. So is smiling when you are talking about something sad or painful. Defense mechanisms are similar to the soft spots we've discussed. They are part of a person's psychological make-up, they are there for a reason, and when something or someone pokes at them or judges them, it hurts—a lot.

Defense mechanisms are our not ideal behavior, especially in an attempt to heal our anxiety wounds. But they are also not malicious or mean. They are a way of distancing oneself from the truth so life gets more tolerable. Personal growth and emotional development lead to lowering one's defense mechanisms, particularly when introspecting. Instead of covering up the authentic truth with certain behaviors, the truth is shared in a genuine and honest (and vulnerable) way. Some of our anxiety responses—and symptoms—are defense mechanisms. Let's talk about a few.

1. Dissociation

I often felt empty-brained. I could feel my mouth moving, acknowledge that I was talking. Still, my mind was far away from the anxiety-provoking event. When I used to engage in a stressful conversation with my ex, this is what usually happened: the discussion got convoluted and I saw myself agreeing to things or going along with something, and at the end of it all, I found myself thinking, "What the hell just happened? What did I just agree to? I don't even understand what just happened …"

"I don't dare to talk to him alone face-to-face as openly as I do in writing. When I'm in front of my computer in a neutral state, I can collect my thoughts much better than when I'm sitting with him in a room. Even the idea of talking releases many stress hormones in me that kind of numb my ability to think clearly. I feel unsafe opening up as I often experience disagreement, withdrawal, or as you pointed out, gaslighting coming my way."—My personal diary, 7th June 2019.

I was so terrified of getting blamed or criticized that my mind just gave up. Have you ever experienced something similar?

In a sense, it's as if one is disconnecting from themself in those moments and responding to something other than their authentic reaction. This behavior is a form of defense called dissociation. You step away from who you are, what you know, what you feel, and what you want. Then, in the moments that follow, you are faced with these questions that you ask of yourself, "What just happened? What did I just agree to …?"

Dissociation is a disconnected state of mind from the here and now. Everyone's mind wanders occasionally, but dissociation in the sense we're exploring it is coping by avoiding pessimistic thoughts or feelings. Dissociation is a form of avoidance, which can lower fear, anxiety, and shame.[v]

Feeling powerless and out of control can lead the mind to disconnect from the situation to cope with helplessness. It helps us get through to the end of the distressing experience. People who learn to dissociate as a response to an anxiety-provoking event are likely to solidify dissociation as a defense mechanism.

If you recognize yourself doing this, it is your emotional challenge to get better acquainted with this process … the stepping away from your authentic self during challenging times. My anxiety was triggered by a serious discussion with a loved one where I knew I would be blamed and my feelings would be dismissed. But other things can provoke the defense mechanism of dissociation too, such as fear of public speaking, taking an exam, doing an activity that's way out of your comfort zone, traumatic events, or re-traumatizing experiences.

The good news is that once you learn more about how this plays out for you (through reading, contemplation, therapy, and/or journaling), you can practice alternative ways of responding to such triggers. You can feel more like you are present and properly representing your true self.

You will need to learn to have a different reaction when you are splitting off or feeling dissociated due to anxiety. Instead of doing the thing you have the tendency to do, you will want to learn and practice a different way of handling the experience.

There are many forms of self-care you could try. The important thing is to find the one that soothes you adequately and fits for how you want to be.

Here are some practices you can do when you experience dissociation:

- Make a clear statement about dissociation. Come up with a word or phrase that you will say when you feel dissociated. "I feel spaced out. I feel like I'm losing ground."
- Remove yourself from the situation. If you are talking with someone, tell them, "I don't feel good right now. Can we talk about this … (choose a time when you think you'd be comfortable resuming the interaction)?"
- Answer the following questions to yourself: "Where am I now? What time is it? What day is it?"

- Take deep breaths to ground yourself. Get familiar with your surroundings. Name five things you see, hear, and touch. Count how many yellow items you can see around you. Name five things, which start with the letter "a," then "b," and so on.

- Stimulate your senses physically. Touch something cold or warm (don't burn yourself). Smell something soothing like lavender or chamomile. Eat something sweet. Massage your temples and neck.[vi]

The following are some questions you can ask yourself when you're in a neutral state of mind to explore your dissociation:

When am I most likely to dissociate? What event/who triggers it?

....
....
....
....

What do you feel when you dissociate? How does it manifest in your body?

....
....
....
....

Brainstorm ways to snap out of the dissociative state of mind. Think about the first symptoms you have. What could you do to nip dissociation in the bud?

....
....
....
....

I wish to highlight that I'm talking about dissociation as a behavioral trait or a defense mechanism, not a diagnosable disorder—mild dissociative episodes that rarely surface and are triggered only by a few particular events. A full-blown dissociative disorder is what used to be referred to as Multiple Personality Disorder (MPD). Now it's referred to as DID or Dissociative Identity Disorder. DID is born out of severe emotional and physical abuse and trauma. People with DID are usually unaware that they are dissociating or "splitting off."

Now, I know this might sound scary, "What if I have a personality disorder?" and you might spiral downward in the rabbit hole of anxiety. If you are quite aware of splitting off, that points to your relatively firm grasp of reality. As with most disorders, there are traits of those disorders that "normal" people possess, without actually having the condition itself. Having a couple of the characteristics, or having many of the traits to a mild degree, doesn't meet the diagnostic criteria for having a full-blown diagnosis of the disorder.

Suppose you feel that you dissociate frequently and aren't aware of it. In that case, you should consider talking to a therapist or psychiatrist. This is not meant to be a diagnostic platform, and dealing with severe dissociation is beyond this book's scope.

2. Rationalization

A classic defense mechanism, rationalization is something all of us do. Can you relate to the following story?

Why didn't I sit down to do the work I was supposed to do? Well ... because I worked so much yesterday, and my brain was literally exhausted. Also, my cousin came over with her three-year-old, and by the time they left, I was even more tired. I had to catch up on the news, and before I knew it, it was one hour past my bedtime. I didn't sleep enough, and also, that wretched neighbor made a terrible noise with his kitchen refurbishing DIY project, which, ahh ... it's just so annoying. I couldn't go out to work in a coffee shop, either, because they only have outdoor seating now due to COVID. Which, by the way, I might have contracted,

I felt a bit feverish in the morning, but now I feel okay ... but I didn't know back then when I was out of groceries. I couldn't go grocery shopping because, duh, I thought I had COVID, right? So I chose to order food. But the restaurant I wanted to order from opened two hours later. So I had to wait. While waiting for my food to arrive, I was so hangry I couldn't have possibly concentrated on work. After I ate, I had to digest. I was so full. One can't work with a full belly. When I finally sat down to work, literally five minutes later, my husband came home and started watching the basketball finals. And you know how fans are when they really get into their game? Loud. He yelled for three hours straight. So ... is it surprising I didn't do it?

No, brain, it's not surprising at all. Now, take a breath, will you?

It sounds familiar, right? We tell ourselves this long story about why we didn't do what we were supposed to in an attempt to ease our anxiety. We know that we're in the wrong; we feel it at a gut level. That knowing creates this friction between our id (I just want to eat and watch *The Bachelorette* all day) and our superego (I need to work to make a good living, like a decent citizen and provide for my family). Our ego, the rational self, tries to appease the other two parts, but the anxiety it feels is just too much. So, rationalization is used to ease the discomfort.

We try to explain the undesired feeling or behavior rationally or logically. In the meantime, we do our best to ignore the real cause behind the emotion or action. For a short time, we feel better, absolving ourselves of our "sin." Rationalization also protects our self-esteem by lowering our anxiety. We believe the story we tell, thus we don't feel so bad about ourselves. But in the long run, whatever we're rationalizing our way out of will gather above our head. There will come the point when no amount of rationalizing will obscure the obvious: we're doing something wrong, or we're not doing what we should.

Here we can respond in one of two ways.

1. When the pain of *not* making the change is more significant than making it, we'll stop rationalizing and do what we need. This is what most people do. They procrastinate and procrastinate until there's no way out of the chore … It's the typical leaving-things-to-the-last-minute mentality.

Living life this way is not the end of the world, but our days can become unnecessarily stressful. Most of us stress and feel anxious while procrastinating. Very few people can lay back and genuinely not give a damn about what they're avoiding. As long as we finish everything we need on time, on the surface, we're not sabotaging our life. If we hand in the paper on the last day, complete the project just before the deadline, we're not going to fail our class or get fired. (Assuming the quality of our work is more or less decent.)

Not everything we rationalize about has a deadline, though. Some things we put off can reach a level of damage where reparation is not possible. Think about relationships. Let's take a look at Lara and Ben. Lara needs affectionate gestures from Ben to feel loved, safe, and fulfilled. She mentions this to Ben a few times, but nothing changes. Over time, she becomes more distant and starts losing faith in the relationship. One day she decides that this is not the way she wants to live, so she goes to Ben, "We need to talk …"

Oh, that sentence.

Ben, not wanting to lose Lara, promises that he'll be more affectionate from now on, but the damage was already done. Lara lost faith and interest in the relationship. She feels she spent too much time already in a situation where she felt her needs were not taken seriously. Ben, of course, feels devastated. He was aware of Lara's needs, but he didn't consider it important. Ben told himself, "Tomorrow, I'll get her some flowers," but he always found something else to do. Ben knew deep down that his relationship was not headed in the right direction. He could feel Lara cooling off around him, but he rationalized his way out of the observation. "Today she had a long day at work. She has her period. Her mom nagged her again." Now that she's packing up her stuff, he'd do anything to make her stay. But listening and caring enough to meet someone's emotional needs doesn't have a strict deadline. Goodwill erodes over time, and on occasions, it can't be regained.

2. Another way to respond to unbearable anxiety is to switch defense strategies. When we can't rationalize ourselves out of something, we use denial to push the anxiety-provoking subject out of our mind. We'll talk more about denial in a bit.

Regardless of our response, leaving things for the last minute or switching to denial, we create many anxiety scars in our hearts—and in our bodies. A stress hormone called cortisol can cause a lot of health complications. When you live your life in constant stress, cortisol is released by the adrenal glands. This hormone triggers "a flood of glucose that supplies an immediate energy source to your large muscles. It also inhibits insulin production, so the glucose won't be stored but available for immediate use. Cortisol narrows the arteries, while another hormone, epinephrine, increases your heart rate. Working together, they force your blood to pump harder and faster as you confront and resolve the immediate threat." While helpful when in real danger, this process can have a series of negative consequences over time. High blood sugar levels, weight gain, suppressed immune system, digestive problems, and heart disease are just a few of the many conditions you can develop living on a constant cortisol high.[vii]

In summary, rationalization may seem like a harmless habit. But weigh in the anxiety and stress it indirectly creates—the increased cortisol level and its detrimental impact on health—and rationalization is definitely something you should avoid.

The key to change is awareness. You need to know precisely what and how you rationalize. Let's think about it together.

What is your main rationalization pattern? What exact sentences, topics, and excuses do you use to avoid taking action or making a change? (For example, "I am tired." "I am not qualified." "I don't have time." "I don't know how …")

....
......
....
......
....
......
....
......

I am prone to rationalizing about these aspects of my life: (For example, finishing work-related tasks ahead of time.)

....
......
....
......
....
......

Now, dig more in-depth about your subjects of rationalization. If we use the work-related tasks as an example, what part exactly makes you hesitant to start working? Is the task too overwhelming? Does it require a lot of research? Is it a topic that you're bored of? Do you hate your boss, and procrastinating is your way of protesting? What exactly triggers you to rationalize?

....
......
....
......
....
......
....
......

What emotion(s) does the subject of your rationalization trigger in you? (Boredom, desperation, overwhelm, annoyance …?)

……………………………………………………
……
……………………………………………………
……
……………………………………………………
……

What can you do to make the subject of your rationalization more appealing? Think of strategies you could employ to stop rationalizing and start doing what you're putting off. (For example, watch a motivational video to get you in the mood. Get rid of distractions. Break down your tasks into bite-sized pieces. Reaffirm the importance of your partner in your life. Do something small to grease the squeaky wheels …)

……………………………………………………
……

How would your life be different if you quit rationalizing and just did what you had to do? Get creative with this one. Explore less-than-immediate, long-term benefits, too.

3. Denial

Denial is another common defense mechanism. When in denial, people refuse to acknowledge that something is wrong in their lives. It is a form of "coping with emotional conflict, stress, painful thoughts, threatening information, and anxiety." People seem unable to face reality or admit an obvious truth. When someone is in denial, they absolutely refuse to accept or see that something has happened or is happening at the moment. Think about drug addicts or alcoholics. Denial lies as a key problem at the center of their addiction. They often categorically reject that they have issues with substance abuse. Or, if they admit that they have been drinking a bit, for example, they can aggressively argue that it's not a big deal.[viii]

In rare cases—and for a short term—denial can actually be helpful. Victims of traumatic events can use denial to protect their psyche from memory. This gives their minds a break to step back and slowly get accustomed to the painful truth. Slow processing prevents mental overwhelm and a potential breakdown. After stepping away, one can get a better grip on reality and arrive at more constructive "What's next?" questions.

The main scope of denial is to protect us from the things we can't deal with or are too uncomfortable to admit. In some cases, people admit their shortcomings or problem but downplay their importance shortly after. Some can grasp reality in all its seriousness, but they will deny their own part in the problem. They will blame others instead. On the surface, this defense mechanism alleviates the pain of anxiety, but it also costs us a lot of effort.

Have you ever suspected your partner cheating for a long time, or settled for a deeply dissatisfying workplace? Whenever people brought to your attention the anomaly of the situation you were in, did you feel this strong urge to tell them wrong? "She is a good woman. She just works overtime. She's hard-working, you know. Greg? He's just a colleague." Or, "My job is the best I can wish for. There's nothing wrong with disliking it."

Denial is a problem if it lingers:

- If you don't go to the doctor after having peed blood for weeks.
- If you don't admit that the death of your sibling significantly affected your life.

- If you accumulate so much credit card debt, you don't even open the notification letters after a time.

- If you ignore that, while your child asks for lunch money every day, she loses weight and smells of tobacco each day.

In the cases mentioned above, denial is very harmful because it prevents you from seeking a solution to significant problems. These issues can spiral out of control and have devastating consequences.

Life can get too much on occasion. It's okay to take a step back and affirm, "This is just too much to take right now," and avoid the subject of distress for a bit. Give yourself the time you need to process and adapt to the new reality you're facing. But remember, just because you avoid the problem, it won't solve itself. The longer you wait, the more trouble you'll have in the future.

Be your own denial police. Now you know about its existence. Evaluate yourself based on the following points, and based on your responses, assess if you're in a state of denial:

- Honestly examine what you fear.
…………………………………………..
…………………………………………..
…………………………………………..

- Think about the potential negative consequences of not taking action.
…………………………………………..
…………………………………………..
…………………………………………..

- Allow yourself to express your fears and emotions.

....
....
....

- Try to identify irrational beliefs about your situation.

....
....
....

- Journal about your experience.
- Open up to a trusted friend or loved one.
- Participate in a support group.[ix]

If you feel that you can't cope with the subject of your denial on your own, consider talking to a therapist. Ask for guidance and coping tips. I don't want to offer too many details here, as denial-related support has to be specifically tailored to your unique problem.

4. Projection

When we're projecting, we ascribe to others the qualities and feelings we can't accept about ourselves. For example, if you feel resentful about someone, you might instead believe this person is resentful towards you. "Projection works by allowing the expression of the desire or impulse, but in a way that the ego cannot recognize, therefore reducing anxiety."[x]

The discomfort that is not brought to conscious awareness can make us ascribe heavy feelings to someone else to avoid fully recognizing it in ourselves. For example, if you were raised that anger and resentment are bad emotions and you consider yourself a good person, you will face a cognitive dissonance when you're angry. To resolve this inner conflict, you'll project your anger onto the other person and believe that they are mad at you. Another classic example is accusing your partner of infidelity when, in fact, you're the one having your eyes set on your coworker.

Projection also includes trait displacement. For example, you attribute the qualities of your ex to your new partner.

My best friend, Hilda, and I talked about her insights about her behavior around Nick, her boyfriend. She feels terrified about Nick finding her boring, so she's trying to be more interesting ... It struck me that she might be projecting there. She experiences him as dull (as we discussed his texting style and their pillow talk). So, with that perception of him, it's as if she is projecting the "I think you're boring" sentiment onto him, making it where he thinks, "I think you're boring," about her. But chances are, that's not even on his radar. That is probably not his thought process. But it is hers.

When Nick is overworked and exhausted, his energy—both physical and emotional—is drained. Not only does a person in his situation not have the power to feel frisky and playful, but he also doesn't have the energy to feel judgmental and critical of Hilda and her level of interesting-ness. In other words, he is experiencing something very different than what she is experiencing. When Hilda may be feeling a little neglected or disconnected, followed by uncertainty and anxiety, Nick's feeling sleep-deprived and physically and mentally exhausted. In those situations, her needs are very different. When she needs connection and attention, he needs rest, sleep, a mental break, and some time to replenish his energy. That makes it challenging when two people are together and their needs are totally different.

I could see how being beside a drained and exhausted person—when she is not feeling that way—could feel a little boring from her perspective. And if that is indeed what she is feeling, that's where the projection would come into play.

Projection is funny that way. You take an emotional experience that belongs to you, and you put it onto another person. How can you get out of this habit? When projection is happening, the goal is to "own it" and say, "That's my stuff," and then "take back the projection." Owning it means being okay with the fact that you have that feeling, rather than feeling anxious about it.

Hilda values being interesting, challenging, and adding value to the person's life with whom she is. These are traits that she finds important, which may explain why it may cut so profoundly when she assumes she's not being enough of these things. These are essential character traits of hers and, indeed, are all really great values. I encourage her if she believes that these are indeed her values, to hold them dear, and make sure she is living her life by them.

That's pretty much what mending projection boils down to—when something is important to you (and you know it is because it causes lots of anxiety when you feel like you're not living up to those things), make sure you are taking action in your life that supports those things.

Hilda should make sure to do things that she finds attractive (by her measurement, not by anyone else's). She needs to take action, so she doesn't get bored with herself or how she is running her life; to make sure she is doing things that satisfy her desire to bring value to others.

If you do not measure up to your own values (again, by your own standards, not by someone else's), then change course and do something different. You're in the driver's seat on this one. Rather than worry that you're not enough in someone else's eyes, be enough—by your standards of enoughness—in your eyes.

An important thing to keep in mind with projection is that the anxiety and the trauma from your past painful emotional experiences belong to you, not the other person. When your fears and insecurities come up, do your best to work on them internally first. When you notice that you're projecting, try talking your problem out with a friend, a therapist, or your journal about it.

5. Sublimation

Some of the things we want in our lives are pretty dark. Some of us secretly fantasize about not working, stealing, or leading parallel lives with multiple people. Yet most of us rarely act on these sorts of desires. We instead pour all that frustration and energy into meaningful projects. We are going out of our way to be good and helpful to those around us. In other words, we can put our primitive, destructive, selfish needs to good use. This is basically what sublimation means; it allows us to act out undesirable emotions by reducing them into a more acceptable version.[xi]

For example, a person experiencing extreme disappointment and rage might take up Thai boxing to release their frustration. In this way, they transform their destructive emotions into something constructive. Many artists who were unhappy and broke used their talents to create something beautiful out of all that suffering. In Sigmund Freud's view, disappointment is inevitable. We'll always long for more things that we can get. But we can transform that frustration using sublimation. Envy can be turned into effort—a wounded heart into being more grateful and empathetic.

Anna Freud considered sublimation a form of maturity, which enabled people to act in socially acceptable ways. In Freud's opinion, psychoanalysis is the tool that can help us find healthy ways to turn our primal, unacceptable cravings into something helpful and socially acceptable. A good life is not about getting everything we want but to find and practice fulfilling alternatives.

There are thoughts and desires in our psyche we can't eradicate. And we shouldn't. Trying to get rid of something will just make the thing stubbornly persistent. Acceptance and, ultimately, sublimation is a good goal to have. We can transform ourselves. We can turn our anxiety into vulnerability.

I felt ashamed about my anxieties and sensitivities for a long time. I believed something was fundamentally wrong with me. My father always appraised me for doing wild, mischievous, or even socially indignant things. He took great pride in doing all those things himself. When I felt overwhelmed by trying to please him with actions so uncomfortable to me, he said, "My daughter is not a scaredy-cat. She is a tomboy!" He had good intentions, of course. This was the way he showed support. But deep down, it just further alienated me from my true self. Then came my ex, who called my anxious-sensitive self outright wrong, undesirable, and abnormal.

Despite all the negative feedback I got about who I was at the core, I decided to use these unacceptable qualities to do something good with them. I decided to write self-help books, to disclose a little more of my true personality, and to embrace my shortcomings even in my books. I decided that I wouldn't claim to be an expert on the things I'm preaching—I am very much a work in progress. I chose to be vulnerable and honest. I think this is a form of sublimation.

Only recently have I discovered the concept of highly sensitive people, to which I could relate completely. Being sensitive to the environment is a blessing and a curse. But one can choose to focus on the blessing aspect of it and do something useful with it.

Now that you've read about sublimation, can you detect instances in your life when you transformed a weakness into an asset? Or when you chose to do something good with an aspect of yourself you once found unacceptable?

....
....

....
....
....
....

Think about your current "shortcomings." These can be thoughts, desires, or traits you're ashamed of or uncomfortable with. How can you embrace them and turn them into life-enhancing power?

....
....
....
....
....
....

In conclusion ...

Can you overcome your defense mechanisms? I believe you can. It will take some time, but you have every chance to overwrite them. Think of it like a person who injured their arm earlier in life. The arm can heal. Perhaps there are some minor limitations around how that arm functions. Maybe it needs some extra TLC in the form of stretching, massage, anti-inflammation salve, and so on, but the person with the old injury can still write, draw, eat with a fork and knife, exercise, and so on as much as they want to. They just have to be mindful of their arm and not subject it to extra stress and strain. Any form of defense mechanism can be worked through. With support, insight, willingness to grow, and practice at managing one's actions in a better way, a person with anxiety and defense mechanisms that protect a wounded psyche can be healed.

Wanting to outgrow your defenses and manage your anxiety says a lot about the path of your life and your own personal growth. Because there once was a time when the defenses were more important and influential than anything else. That's precisely why they got constructed in the first place. But you reached a point in your life and in your emotional development where the defenses are no longer serving you as they did when they were first constructed. Not only are they not serving you, but they are actually costing you …

Affirm to yourself, "I've outgrown the need for these defenses, and they are no longer serving me the way they used to, so I need to shed them to open my life to better things."

Chapter 5: Abandonment Anxiety

I used to be—and to some extent, still am—very much afraid of being abandoned by my partner. When abandonment issues are strong and powerful, they become the driving force for other life areas, particularly pertaining to romantic relationships.

For some people, if you ask them, "What's the worst thing that'll happen to you if somebody leaves you?" their answer might be, "I'll be sad," or, "I'll be lonely, I'll be depressed for a while."

For people with profoundly entrenched abandonment anxiety, if you ask them to honestly answer what the worst thing that'll happen to them if they get left by a significant other is, they might be quick to say, "I will die." Not that they would, but the feeling is there, the feeling that they will not survive without the other.

People who say that don't actually believe they will die; their intellect can tell them that they will make it, as they have made it in the past. Yet if any part of your emotional make-up is operating with this belief system, you'll want to give that some extra attention right away. Trying to save ourselves from being abandoned at all costs can bring us much anxiety and unfulfillment in life.

Imagine a drowning man who is splashing around and expending all his energy. He believes he will die. He reacts to the anxiety of facing his death, rather than setting that aside and managing the current situation with calmness and easy, gentle movements and steady breathing. This metaphor translates well to what we do when our abandonment anxiety is triggered. We cling, fight, feeling nauseated, choking on our fear … It's not a matter of, "I am going to die," but it is a case of, "I am losing ground, I am losing them, I am being abandoned and rejected, I am failing …"

Having anxiety in reaction to these conditions is totally normal, of course. Anyone would. It's not the anxiety that is off base. It's the conclusion that all these bad things are actually happening—that is usually off base.

When you're feeling like you're losing your power, you're losing control, you're losing ground … it's good to ask yourself, "Is this really happening to me? Or am I merely assuming this is happening to me? Do I really know, for sure? Is there more information needed to know for sure?" The answer we usually give, once we calm down, is not what our anxious mind created. This being said, there are self-sabotaging behaviors which can lead to abandonment. Let's take a look at one of them.

I will tell you a story that I have repeated multiple times in my life. It is hard to even recall it as I caused myself a lot of pain following this pattern. Yet, in the past, I was not consciously aware of my behavior. I just felt victimized by my ex-partners. Looking back, a lot of my misery was caused by my own lack of self-knowledge and self-love. I hope to help you recognize a maladaptive behavior pattern that took me 14 years to pinpoint.

"What will he think of me? Am I pretty, hot, sexy enough? Am I smart, interesting, challenging enough? Sporty enough? Cool enough?" These questions circled my mind like a hungry hawk orbits over its prey. Whenever I did or said something wrong, my mental hawk slammed down my inadequacy prey and tore it apart with its sharp beak. I was so harsh on myself. I wanted to be harsh first, before my partner at the time could be. In my head, if I allowed him to see how flawed I was, I'd lose him. He'd go find someone better. So, my mission was to not let anything terrible slip. And as you can imagine, I mainly chose partners who were highly critical and hard to please.

Over time, I developed a heightened sense of anxiety because of the enormous fear of abandonment, and masqueraded it as perfectionism. I'd go to the gym five times a week to stay in shape. I'd regularly visit beauty salons. I'd wake up ten minutes before my boo to do my makeup, brush my teeth, and I'd sneak back into the bed to "wake up" as actresses do in Hollywood movies, flawlessly. I'd work hard to have my own money and not seem like a gold digger. I'd read the news to be smart and up-to-date. I'd cook. I'd surprise them every day. I'd be generous with compliments … The list is long. I did so much to maintain my perfect façade because I felt so imperfect. And imperfection meant losing love. And losing love meant … that I wouldn't survive.

Can you relate to this story? Have you ever gone out of your way to please your partner so that they wouldn't leave you and wouldn't criticize you?

And then, despite doing all that work, inevitably, you made a "mistake." Your partner was very observant (aka critical) and told you about your flaw. You'd feel like they just hammered a nail in your heart halfway, and you'd make sure that you'd bang that bloody nail deeper, criticizing yourself, too. Then you'd try to please even harder, with even higher levels of anxiety until you couldn't carry the burden any longer … You exploded. For twenty minutes, you allowed all that bottled up frustration, fear, and rage to bubble up and have a free flow. In these instances, you didn't use the vocabulary your mom would be proud of.

When your rage was consumed, you became terrified of what you'd done. Your partner was in shock, felt victimized, and undeservedly lashed out at. They may or may not have done something to provoke it, stepping on one of your anxiety buttons, but in the big picture of things, they were right. They didn't deserve the treatment they got. And you knew it. You knew deep down that it was not their fault you felt so exhausted being perfect. It was you, at the end of the day, who forced perfection onto yourself, not them. But deep inside you also knew that all of it was necessary; otherwise, the inevitable abandonment would have happened already.

Your anxiety, nevertheless, goes through the roof, "Now I did it. Now my partner will surely leave me." You promise that this won't happen again, and you jump back on your mission to be even more perfect than before. You work much harder now, as you know you've done something wrong. Before long, your anxiety tank fills up again, and you lash out again.

The more you repeat this pattern, the more scars you leave on your partner, who doesn't feel like they deserve the treatment they're getting. They scar you back with words and slowly become more distant. This further triggers your anxiety and fear of abandonment. So, the entire process described above escalates, and eventually does lead to a breakup. This is a classic case of self-sabotage, a self-fulfilling prophecy.

The story above is just one of the many ways unattended abandonment wounds can create a lot of damage in your life. Fear of any kind gives birth to anxiety. As we learned, we adopt a series of defense mechanisms to protect against this anxiety. Can you see how many unconscious layers hide beneath our actions? Let's break this onion down.

Stage One: The Victim Zone

Lara is not self-aware and lives reactively, usually feeling victimized. "I don't know why this happens to me ALL THE TIME. The guy is interesting and interested. And I do SO MUCH for him. And then I make a little mistake, and he gets more distant. He doesn't appreciate me. I feel so resentful. But I love him so much, I don't want him to leave me. Maybe I didn't do my very best, so I'm going to try better now."

Lara is trapped in a reinforcing loop: trying too hard, making a mistake, feeling criticized/resentful, trying harder out of fear of abandonment while having less patience due to resentment, and then making another mistake …

Lara always feels that life is conspiring against her. She only knows that she tries so hard, yet she fails to keep a relationship every single time. She may draw one of two conclusions over time in stage one. On one hand, she'd start to believe that all men leave. Men are not to be trusted. All of them are jerks. On the other hand, she might turn on herself, buying into the conviction that something is fundamentally wrong with her. She is simply not made for having a relationship. People at this stage usually feel sad and powerless.

Stage Two: The Defense Debunk

Lara recognizes that she has very high standards for herself—goals impossible to meet—but she feels there's nothing to do about them. The defense is a fundamental part of her identity; she doesn't look at it as a defense mechanism but something that she is (sometimes even proud of). "I know I am a perfectionist. I can't help it. That's just who I am ... I can't change. I mean, my mom was like that all the time, and she never changed either. It's just me. Besides, there's nothing wrong with striving for my best self, right? If the guy can't see and appreciate that ... well ... I have to try better. I don't want him to leave me. I love him so much."

In stage two, people have some self-awareness and don't perceive themselves as a total victim. The defense mechanism of perfectionism, in this case, mixes up with rationalization (there's nothing wrong about striving for my best self). It gets sprinkled with some denial (I can't help it. That's who I am) and defensiveness (my mom was like that all the time). People at this stage usually feel anger.

Stage Three: Anxiety Awareness

Lara got very angry one day, so she sat down to dig deeper into her anger in some books. She discovered that her perfectionism could be triggered by anxiety. She recognizes that the all-too-familiar feeling of mental numbness, tightness in her throat and chest, and the difficulty of taking deep breaths all point toward anxiety. "I can't believe it! Whenever I think about Ben, these physical sensations possess my body and prompt me to quickly fix dinner, send a hot picture, or a cute text. I do feel anxious before, during, and after almost everything I do to impress Ben …"

Stage three is an excellent place to be because, if someone gets here, it's only a matter of time before they will start asking why. "Why am I feeling this way? Why am I so anxious? What triggers my anxiety?" This is the stage where one's attention shifts inward and starts to look for answers from there. The dominant emotion here is curiosity.

Stage Four: Childhood Shit

Lara went down the rabbit hole of memory lane and discovered that the anxiety she feels around Ben is not new. She felt the same way every time she interacted with her cold, overly critical father. He didn't make it a secret about always wanting a boy instead of a girl. Lara had to fight for her father's love all her childhood, trying very hard to be the boy her dad never had. Of course, this was a failed mission from the start. When she was seven, her parents divorced, and she didn't see her dad ever again. Lara had a massive hole in her heart. For no good reason, she never felt enough for her dad, and despite her best attempts, her dad ended up leaving her.

Ever since then, she tried to fill that hole with men who quite simply wanted something else than what she was. For example, Ben told her that he loves independent, self-assured women (which Lara pretended to be in the beginning). By nature, Lara was a more emotional and insecure being, who found genuine fulfillment in mutual dependence. Ben could never fulfill that need as he was a different personality. Lara also couldn't meet Ben's needs as she was not what he expected. In the first three stages, however, Lara was not self-aware enough to see this. She couldn't connect the dots; she didn't know why she did the things she did. In stage four, all that became crystal clear. She was reenacting her childhood trauma with her father over and over again. The primary emotion of stage four is shock.

Stage Five: The Leap

The distance between stages four and five requires the most significant jump. Why? Because up to stage four, every observation and discovery we make is internal. Our life doesn't change tangibly just because we know what we know. Stage five is the layer of taking action. Lara has to affirm to herself that she has abandonment-related fear. This fear stems from her relationship with her father and influences her romantic choices. She realizes that the fear of abandonment leaves her very anxious, and this anxiety triggers different defenses such as perfectionism. But now she can clearly see how the behavior created to save the relationship actually alienated it.

She sees that when, as a little kid, she adopted her defense mechanisms, she fought a life-or-death fight as her survival depended on having her father around. Her father leaving was not a personal failure of hers. It was never about her. She also sees that now. The defense was meant to protect her, but it is clear now that it's keeping her from what she truly wants. It is also apparent why.

What happened with her father was never Lara's fault. Neither is she to blame for the defense system she created as a child. But now, as a self-aware adult, it is her responsibility to take inventory of the maladaptive behavior she needs to change and the overgrown expectations she needs to adjust. Ultimately, she has to decide to change her ways of relating to men and commit to living the life she desires and deserves.

Stage Six: Awakened Life

Lara works hard to get to know herself at this stage of awareness, to become familiar with her triggers, her reactions, and the red flags she ignored before. She uses her journal to collect data about her general conduct. She makes little notes for herself as reminders of what she needs to do or should avoid doing. She takes some time off from the dating scene to solidify the changes she's working hard to change. And then, suddenly, she meets someone different. Luke may not seem so exciting at first as

Ben was, but he is caring, present, and accepts Lara as she is. Lara knows that there is no point in pretending to be someone else than she truly is. She shows her authentic self to Luke, warts and all. And Luke wants her. Wants *her*. She never felt wanted like this before. As their relationship slowly deepens, her scars, one by one, start to heal.

It may seem that Luke is the one who healed Lara's heart. But it was Lara who first found and accepted herself. She made the commitment to not repeat the story she always played. It was her who, even though it was terrifying, let Luke see her authentic self. She allowed Luke to accept her by allowing herself to be seen. Luke's healing power wouldn't have been possible if Lara hadn't made space for it first.

Along the way of life, we who have abandonment scars develop a mechanism for ensuring that we will not be abandoned. We often develop a persona who wants to meet their partner's every need, even when our own needs aren't being met. Making your partner feel good is our strategy for minimizing the risk of, or preventing altogether, abandonment. The bigger the abandonment issues, the more a person is willing to "do anything" to avoid abandonment from occurring.

Overcoming abandonment issues is a long-haul proposition. Not to say that good headway can't be made right away, because it certainly can. But this is one of those topics that is so deeply intertwined into our emotional make-up. It will take some unraveling to get to a place of completely letting go of it, or being "healed." Three-steps-forward-two-steps-back progression is a realistic expectation for healing our abandonment wounds. Even though we know better, we'll still make mistakes; we'll still feel anxiety, which will still prompt us into defensive behavior. It may not be the same defense mechanism we used before. But learning to trust that, even if we are abandoned, we are still going to be okay, is a long journey.

You're at a place in your life now where you're being asked to grow. You are here, and I know that you'll put in the work. This—in an odd and very uncomfortable way—is a gift. Understanding how your abandonment triggers work can help you grasp why you feel anxious and irritated for "no reason." Noticing your triggers gives you a chance to bring awareness and compassion to your mind's fear response. It can help you release some of the shame around your reaction and develop solutions on how to handle your anxiety.

If you recognized that you're having abandonment issues, it means that you're at least at stage four of self-awareness. Are you ready to take the leap to stage five?

Addressing abandonment issues starts with bringing the case out of the shadows and into the conversational light, as we have done. And it continues by getting as closely acquainted with your process as possible, knowing yourself and what you're doing, and why you're doing it.

You want to get a clear picture of what you do to maintain your relationship's security.

What are the "manipulations" you have learned to do? What have your strategies been?

……………………………………………………
………
……………………………………………………
………
……………………………………………………
………
……………………………………………………
………

We have mentioned many of these strategies already. Perfectionism, denial, and defensiveness are some of them. But passive aggression or more insidious emotionally abusive tools can be at work, too. Gaslighting, shifting the goalpost, or trying to diminish the other's self-esteem to feel more secure about your own could also pop up. You want to make sure you are uncovering all of them. Some of them may not be pretty. It's okay. There's nothing you can't change if you truly desire, but it's crucial to detect all of them. It's what they refer to in twelve-step programs as "taking a fearless moral inventory." You want to bring all the abandonment-prevention tactics into your conscious awareness and be able to identify and describe them to yourself.

Another part of working on abandonment issues has to do with examining the worst-case scenario. Here you focus on all the things that could or would happen if/when you get abandoned. This is another inventory, only it's a little more under the surface. Some of these thoughts/feelings/beliefs might be more like a software program running in the background, not necessarily part of your conscious thought process. But here, you want to really dig deep and come up with every possible concern or perspective you live with about being abandoned by your relationship partner. Some of these items will be kept alive more by your inner child than your adult mind. It doesn't matter who's bringing them. If they're part of your psyche, they count.

What scares you about being abandoned? Write down everything that comes to mind.

……………………………………………………
………
……………………………………………………
………
……………………………………………………
………
……………………………………………………
………

....
....

A third thing to look at in dealing with abandonment issues is to use your imagination to see if you can come up with how a person who doesn't have abandonment issues might think about the idea of their partner leaving them.

What perspective might they have? How might they look at the whole idea of their relationship coming to a close? What thoughts run through their mind?

....
....
....
....
....
....

....
....

This particular exercise takes some creativity because you're asking yourself to think in a way that is 180 degrees different than how you think. So, it's a case of allowing yourself to step into the shoes of someone who operates totally differently than you do. What might that be like? What might their perspective be when they don't harbor any big fears about being left? Can you imagine …?

Take your time to answer these questions. Sometimes you'll need multiple days to complete a list. That's okay. Just open your journal and jot down every time something new comes up. Overcoming abandonment-related anxiety is a marathon. You need to build up your self-knowledge from stage one upwards. But it's worth the trouble. The reward is self-confidence, peace of mind, and ultimately having the relationship you want.

Finally, walk through the six stages of awareness using your main anxiety trigger in your life. It doesn't have to be abandonment, but whatever you personally feel more anxious about. What stage would you say you're at with your problem? Considering what you know about these stages, design ways to reach stage six:

……………………………………………
……………………………………………
……………………………………………
……………………………………………
……………………………………………
……………………………………………

Chapter 6: The Art of Self-Soothing

You may be thinking that anxiety will always be a small part of your life. You may be right. But the good news is that you can get really good at managing it and not letting it take over your thoughts or moods. In the previous chapter, I touched on how dysfunctional relationships can trigger our anxiety scars. We shield ourselves with creative defense mechanisms, and down the spiral we go. I focused on romantic relationships, but I could have given a friend or family member as an example. In this chapter, I will present healing and loving ways to approach your anxiety within your relationships. We will explore how to cultivate self-acceptance.

A large part of successful anxiety management is self-care. What is self-care? You know, I often wondered that when I came across this concept. My therapist told me to do it. I read in books and heard in podcasts to do it. I felt frustrated and clueless … I didn't know what this concept meant on a practical level.

It made me realize I never learned to care for myself, to soothe myself. Neither of my caregivers knew how to do it. They never did it themselves. My mother, father, and grandparents were very reactive. In a way, they were genuine—whatever they felt came up to the surface. If they felt happy, their eyes would radiate all the joy in the world. But if they were angry, sad, or resentful, those emotions surfaced as well, without any constraint on them. The best takeaway I could get, therefore, was reactivity. For a long time, I thought the way I handled (?) my emotions was absolutely the best way. Only later in life did I learn that just because we feel something, we can't unleash that feeling and expect people around us to just absorb the shock. We can go on without the relationship being affected negatively.

Once I left my family's nest, I was almost stunned by how unreceptive the world was to my emotional management. For some reason, I always felt people mistreated me; my classmates, my distant relatives, my partners … everybody was wrong, only I was right. Stage one of awareness; that's where I was stuck for a long time. The emotional "management" skills I learned from home were terrible. They worked within the closed family system. My grandparents and parents were caught up in unhealthy ways of relating to each other. They were used to hurting each other, to feeling pain. Because they scarred each other every time, they let their wildest emotions loose. Looking back, my heart aches for them ... They were trapped in a cycle of pain to which they got all too accustomed. My grandparents died without ever realizing that they were trapped at stage one in emotional management and self-care.

The moral of this story is ... just because you learned some self-management patterns at home and for a long time you considered them "the way it should be," doesn't mean you can't do better. I learned this lesson the hard way. A lot of people had to push me away, criticize, or abandon me to finally wake up and ask myself the question:

Why? What's my contribution to what's happening to me?

Answer this question, too. Think about an aspect of yourself that often gets you in trouble. It can be explosive emotions, impatience, dishonesty, whatever you feel as though it's not quite the best of your make-up. Ask yourself: "What's my contribution to what's happening to me?"

....
......
....
......
....
......

Knowing your part in a problem is actually powerful. Counterintuitively, it decreases anxiety. I think what causes anxiety around our maladaptive self-regulation is that we don't understand why the world is "out there to get us." We are only doing what we learned to do. But once we actually realize the problematic part of our behavior, we can choose to change that. So we shift from "life happens to me" to "I have control over my life." The sense of control, the sense of ownership, most of the time this releases anxiety.

Back to self-regulation ... Early in life, we should learn a healthy blueprint of self-care from our family. Suppose our caregivers adequately respond to our needs, rock us when we're upset, feed us when we're hungry, cuddle us up in a cozy blanket. In that case, we'll know what gives us comfort later in life. This is the part where they tend to our needs in a caring way. The other part of their task is to show us a good example of how they manage their own emotions and shortcomings. When parents apologize to their children for being unreasonable, harsh, or snappy, they will send positive feedback. The child will learn that it's okay to make mistakes. As long as you reach out and sincerely apologize, the relationship can be mended. But if the parent guilt-trips the child, saying, "Look what you did, you made me so angry," avoiding responsibility, and keeping the child at a distance, the child will learn to be anxious (afraid of losing the parent's love). Also, they will learn to blame others for their emotions and discount any accountability. Ideally, the parent teaches the child to self-care by (1) being attuned to the child's needs, and (2) being a role model in self-management.

Unfortunately, if we didn't receive both of the two parental support methods, we had to learn to care for ourselves in other ways.

These ways are not always good for us. Some people use food, substances, or possessions to comfort themselves. These coping strategies are all stimulants. Good self-care calms the nervous system, opens our heart to put things in perspective, and helps to calm an angry, explosive mind. In good relationships, this skill is essential; to be able to step away and take a break from a fight instead of jumping in. Unleashing our emotions onto the other prompts us to do and say things we later regret.

Think about what comforts you. What are the activities that wind you down? Can you think about five things you did as a child—or at any time in your life—that made you peaceful, centered, and comforted? Write them down.

....
......
....
......
....
......
....
......
....
......

Done? Five things that proved to be soothing in your life are an excellent start to have an idea of what self-care actually looks like. It is not about buying the Burberry bag you always craved or going to an expensive spa. It usually includes something along the lines of taking a bubble bath, snuggling a cozy blanket in bed, reading a good book, listening to relaxing music, talking to a friend, exercising, lighting a candle …

Think about simple things that bring you to a safe place.

You can resort to these self-soothing activities whenever you feel you need it. You can express your need for space when you feel overwhelmed. However, the best way to take care of yourself is to adopt the activities that please you and incorporate them into your regular daily routines. Like I mentioned with other anxiety-management practices, if you start practicing when you're already anxious, it will be challenging to achieve the desired outcome. Practicing self-care on an ongoing basis will fill up your internal reservoir with calming, loving self-care acts. You will be much more grounded, more likely to navigate the waves of anxiety with more ease. It is like preventative medicine. If you are stable at the core, triggers are less likely to get under your skin.

What can you do when you get triggered, and intense anxiety arises? The first element of managing your anxiety is to explore what happens to your relationship with yourself when you're entering into an "anxiety spiral." Think about a recent event and try to answer this question.

………………………………………………
……
………………………………………………
……
………………………………………………
……

What would happen if you stopped (during the anxiety) and looked at yourself in the mirror, right in the eyes, and said, "Hey, sweetheart, what's going on with you? Do you know I love you? Do you know you're loveable? Do you know I got your back?" What would the outcome be if you were to nurture yourself and talk sweetly to yourself as you were spiraling into the negative thinking that goes with anxiety? Try to write some sentences of self-soothing using your own words:

....
......
....
......
....
......

What if you admitted to yourself, "You are a needy, anxious, desperate little thing right now, aren't you ... and I love you anyway ... You're so sweet and cute and loveable, and I don't care if you feel totally inadequate right now, 'cause I love you anyway."

You would want your partner, parent, or friend to be sweet and kind like that, right? You know what it feels like to be on the receiving end of the opposite of that … So now it's time to get good at practicing self-love. When you do it for yourself, other people do it for you, too.

Keep in mind that when it comes to positive self-talk and self-soothing it's okay to admit that you're needy, clingy, anxious, fearful, or insecure … as long as you can say to yourself that you love yourself anyway. If you're secretly saying, "I hate this about you!" there is some healing work to be done.

The same process happens in long-lasting relationships. We arrive to a deeper commitment level, passing the phase of dopamine and oxytocin swirling around in our bloodstream. When we've seen most of our partner's flaws and imperfections, and we can honestly say, "I don't care, I love you anyway!" we know this relationship is meant to be. The same is valid for interacting with ourselves. The "I love you anyway" is the key. Otherwise known as self-acceptance.

Learn to Ask for More Information

There is another big anxiety trigger we haven't mentioned yet: it is living with assumptions. One of my friends often used to say, "Assumptions are the death of facts." This couldn't be more true in the case of our self-generated anxiety. How often have you allowed yourself to spiral from, "He didn't say hi to me," to, "He hates me!" Then add,

"I know this because last time we met, I accidentally pushed him, and now he thinks I'm a raging psycho." When in reality, he doesn't even remember the push, and last time he didn't notice you because he was preoccupied with his investments.

And this is just an assumption we fabricated around a distant acquaintance. How often do we attach catastrophe stories around what our partner does—or doesn't do? For example, we feel a bit under the weather, and we desperately need a good hug with an "I love you," but for some reason, our partner is glued to the TV. As our partner is not a mind reader, our needs can often be unmet in the absence of a request. The trick is, what meaning do we attach to this?

In the absence of genuine information about whether you are being loved, valued, appreciated, desired, and so on … there is anxiety. There is fear that you are losing ground. Without confirmation of those things you need (everyone needs), it's easy to jump to conclusions, to say, "This is bad!" and to get anxiety as a result. You might assume that asking for these needs to be met would make you look needy, overly emotional, and so on. You don't want to be the drama generator. Living without drama is a good goal. But the drama, in this case, is the not-knowing. All you really want is a sense of security.

You'll want to get good at asking for what you need to know; to fill in the gaps in your mind where anxiety tends to fill in. You'll want to practice asking questions that sound authentic, pure, gentle, even vulnerable, and with childlike curiosity instead of questions that sound like an interrogation or loaded with hidden intentions. You want to ask genuine questions about how someone thinks and feels (about you) without them ever feeling defensive or leery of why you are requesting. So, there is an art to that. And I think it is something you can learn to do well, with the right intention.

Let's take a look at some examples of how you can ask for more information from a place of authenticity.

One of the simplest ways of asking for clarification is the question, "What do you mean?" And without adding your interpretation into the picture, allow the other person to explain themselves. This question can come in handy when we feel that heart-stabbing hurt in our chest following someone's remark. Especially if you are familiar with the person, and you know they didn't mean to hurt you. It is of a high likelihood that you two got lost in emotional translation. Asking "What do you mean?" usually clears up the misunderstanding and can even deepen the relationship, adding a new layer of knowledge about the other person. "Isn't it fascinating that what they said meant this to them instead of that?"

If you still don't feel like you understood the other person after the first round of explanation, clarify which part you need further elaboration on.

When you want to express a need instead of asking clarifying questions, it is good to keep in mind that the other person is not in the same emotional state. Others don't attach the same meaning to words or events. With that in mind, approach the other person with kindness. Avoid finger-pointing. Instead of saying, "You're making me feel so terrible by watching the TV all day long!" try, "Could you have some time for me tonight without watching the TV? I'd like to be with you."

Remember that the other person is another feeling human being with flaws and insensitivities. Beyond any kind of behavior, there is a need to feel loved, connected, validated, or comforted. When our partner watches TV, they probably seek comfort. When we talk loudly or snap, we want to mask our insecurity. When we give unsolicited advice, we wish to connect, a need to feel useful. Nothing people do or say to us is purely personal. Try to find the need of your partner when they do something you disapprove of. And just as well, try to find your need behind yours. While some actions and words come off as unskillful, they are rarely initiated with a malicious intention.

Focus on creating closeness instead of distance when you inquire about information or express a need. Notice the difference between the two. How does it feel in your body when you stop the anxiety spiral by asking good, clarifying questions?

....
......
....
......
....
......

The takeaway from this is that you can always ask for more information from another person before deciding you know better what they think and feel, especially if what you believe they think and feel is something that brings anxiety or angst.

Getting more information is a useful technique for managing anxiety, especially anxiety that involves "stinkin' thinking" or endless ruminating and obsessing. So, you may find yourself asking, "What do you mean …" a lot, going forward. And that's okay. It's a much better form of communication than jumping to conclusions, assuming you know, and then feeling bad about it.

Releasing assumptions from your life is a form of self-care. You are prioritizing your mental calm over knee-jerk assumptions. Going the extra mile, asking additional questions for clarification, is more troublesome than just allowing the mind to jump wherever it wants. But it saves a lot of energy and heartache in the long run.

Own Your Stuff

The last self-care practice I'd like to talk about is the practice of owning your own stuff. What does this mean?

You will get good, over time as your self-awareness evolves, at being able to declare what is "your stuff" sooner rather than later as you are in conversations/conflicts with other people. You will distinguish what is a "you issue" and take full responsibility for it.

For example, money was a loaded topic in your family. Your father didn't like to earn money, but he liked to spend it, which put the family in constant deficit. Your partner also likes to spend their money—which is a giant hot button for you. A reaction coming from a lack of self-awareness to this similarity would be criticizing your partner for their irresponsible behavior, creating distance and conflict between the two of you. A reaction from a self-aware place would include noticing the discomfort around your partner's habit, and acknowledging the similarities between them and your dad. But also telling yourself that your partner actually makes more money than your dad did. They save up most of it and spend only what's left after everything is done to secure the family's financial future.

Being able to make this distinction and not react to a salted anxiety wound is what it means when you're "owning your stuff." Money management is a tricky topic for you, but it's ultimately your baggage. You can open up to your partner about your father's spending habits and explain to them your relationship with money from a place of vulnerability and softness. But blaming and being critical is not a good strategy.

And you'll be able to clearly distinguish the "us issues." These are the problematic dynamics in a romantic—or another kind of—relationship. Both parties create them, and fixing them is both of your responsibility.

Let me give you an example of an "us issue."

Your boyfriend is a jolly fellow who sometimes can be relatively insensitive with his jokes. The other day, for example, he made a joke about the way you speak.

Unknowingly, he touched a soft spot, as you've felt very insecure about your speaking style all your life. It's only funny if both of you are laughing, right? So, in this case, your responsibility is to bring your hurt to his attention in a non-attacking, thoughtful way. "When you said that about my way of speaking, it really hurt me." Focus on your experience, not on him. His responsibility is, assuming that he cares about your feelings and doesn't want to hurt you, tuning back on those types of jokes.

Being assertive and standing up for ourselves, however, doesn't come that easy, does it? People who are more anxious than average tend to overanalyze the consequences of protecting their boundaries. (Speaking up for yourself is, in fact, honoring your boundaries.)

Let me ask you a question. Do you feel the need to continually explain yourself when you speak up for yourself or declare your needs? Do you feel more comfortable when you articulate why you need the things you need or why you feel the way you feel? "When you said that about my speaking, it really hurt me ... because when I was in third grade, a classmate made a stand-up comedy show from all the words I pronounced incorrectly, including my stuttering and ... so please, please don't do that to me. It's because of that."

It's natural that we want to explain ourselves, to give a list of supporting arguments for our needs. In a way it makes us feel less imposing. But as time goes by, you will learn to get good at quickly saying, "This is what I need." And to be able to state this without an agenda, or feeling awkward.

You will arrive at this place where you are not compelled in any way to squeeze any sympathy or comfort out of the other person for how rough things have been. That would be the victim card.

With practice, you will have so much more intellectual awareness of your pain, fears, and defenses. The next critical piece is taking full ownership of your pain, past experiences, and outlook on life/people/relationships. Ensure that you're not secretly expecting the other person to somehow make up for those past injustices. It's not on them; it's not their job.

You want to arrive at the place of wanting to clean up the messes that others have made by inflicting pain on your heart. Those hurtful or scary things that happened to you are not fair now, and weren't fair then. Yet it's also unfair to make other people in the present day jump through hoops to prove how they are "not like the others." This way, you'll genuinely own your stuff.

In conclusion …

Your task is to look at how you perceive things, how you think, and the conclusions you tend to draw. Become one who gathers information. Rather than just "knowing" what you are seeing and hearing, you look at it as a scientist and seek more information. To do that, you have to first acknowledge that your truth—the way you see things—isn't necessarily the absolute truth of the world. There are other reasons and explanations for things besides what you know. Make it a quest for knowledge—a search for the truth. Seek to understand, and seek to be understood … as a believer of 7

Habits of Highly Effective People would say.

Final Words

Managing your anxiety is your job as an adult. It was your parents' job when you were a kid, but now it's your job. If your parents didn't do well with that, two things happen: (1) You don't really know how to look out for your own emotional needs and how to soothe your anxious heart, and (2) you feel a little angry about having to learn to take care of your anxiety wounds now, because no one did it for you when they were supposed to.

So first, acknowledge and know what causes you anxiety. Second, assess your situation. Are your needs being met? Are they able to be met? Are you familiar with the tools to soothe your anxiety? (After reading this book, you should have one or two ideas.)

If yes, continue on the path you are on right now, be diligent in your self-learning process, and be kind to yourself.

If not, you can get mad and frustrated at the world and other people, but that is a helpless victim's stance that will not bring you closer to happiness. In fact, it will do the opposite.

So, if you assess what triggers your anxiety and that your needs are not being met, it's up to you—not others—to make the shifts you need in your life. That can mean so many things. Focus on what things you can say and do today. Build yourself up from there.

Learn to express your thoughts and concerns in writing first, then out loud with supportive, trustworthy people. Have them dispel the beliefs you hold—in this case, that your anxiety makes you somehow abnormal.

It's really been an amazing journey we had in this book. I hope you were able to express your deepest concerns and anxieties in your journal and can find answers and practices that help you neutralize them. Keep this up, and you're going to run out of anxieties!

I believe in you!

Love,

Zoe

Before You Go…

How did you like The Healing Power of Journaling? Would you consider leaving a feedback about your reading experience so other readers could know about it? If you are willing to sacrifice some of your time to do so, there are several options you can do it:

1. Please leave a review on Amazon.
2. Please leave a review on goodreads.com. Here is a link to my profile where you find all of my books.
https://www.goodreads.com/author/show/14967542.Zoe_McKey

3. Send me a private message to zoemckey@gmail.com
4. Tell your friends and family about your reading experience.

Your feedback is very valuable to me to assess if I'm on the good path providing help to you and where do I need to improve. Your feedback is also valuable to other people as they can learn about my work and perhaps give an independent author as myself a chance. I deeply appreciate any kind of feedback you take time to provide me.

Thank you so much for choosing to read my book among the many out there. If you'd like to receive an update once I have a new book, you can subscribe to my newsletter at www.zoemckey.com. You'll get Self-Discovery Starter Kit for FREE. You'll also get occasional book recommendations from other authors I trust and know they deliver good quality books.

Other books by Zoe McKey

Brave Enough

Time to learn how to overcome the feeling of inferiority and achieve success. Brave Enough takes you step by step through the process of understanding the nature of your fears, overcome limiting beliefs and gain confidence with the help of studies, personal stories and actionable exercises at the end of each chapter.

Say goodbye to fear of rejection and inferiority complex once and for all.

Less Mess Less Stress

Don't compromise with your happiness. "Good enough" is not the life you deserve - you deserve the best, and the good news is that you can have it. Learn the surprising truth that it's not by doing more, but less with Less Mess Less Stress.

We know that we own too much, we say yes for too many engagements, and we stick to more than we should. Physical, mental and relationship clutter are daily burdens we have to deal with. Change your mindset and live a happier life with less.

Minimalist Budget

Minimalist Budget will help you to turn your bloated expenses into a well-toned budget, spending on exactly what you need and nothing else.

This book presents solutions for two major problems in our consumer society: (1) how to downsize your cravings without having to sacrifice the fun stuff, and (2) how to whip your finances into shape and follow a personalized budget.

Rewire Your Habits

Rewire Your Habits discusses which habits one should adopt to make changes in 5 life areas: self-improvement, relationships, money management, health, and free time. The book addresses every goal-setting, habit building challenge in these areas and breaks them down with simplicity and ease.

Tame Your Emotions

Tame Your Emotions is a collection of the most common and painful emotional insecurities and their antidotes. Even the most successful people have fears and self-sabotaging habits. But they also know how to use them to their advantage and keep their fears on a short leash. This is exactly what my book will teach you – using the tactics of experts and research-proven methods.

Emotions can't be eradicated. But they can be controlled.

The Art of Minimalism

The Art of Minimalism will present you 4 minimalist techniques, the bests from around the world, to give you a perspective on how to declutter your house, your mind, and your life in general. Learn how to let go of everything that is not important in your life and find methods that give you a peace of mind and happiness instead.

Keep balance at the edge of minimalism and consumerism.

The Critical Mind

If you want to become a critical, effective, and rational thinker instead of an irrational and snap-judging one, this book is for you. Critical thinking skills strengthen your decision making muscle, speed up your analysis and judgment, and help you spot errors easily.

The Critical Mind offers a thorough introduction to the rules and principles of critical thinking. You will find widely usable and situation-specific advice on how to critically approach your daily life, business, friendships, opinions, and even social media.

The Disciplined Mind

Where you end up in life is determined by a number of times you fall and get up, and how much pain and discomfort you can withstand along the way. The path to an extraordinary accomplishment and a life worth living is not innate talent, but focus, willpower, and disciplined action.

Maximize your brain power and keep in control of your thoughts.

In The Disciplined Mind, you will find unique lessons through which you will learn those essential steps and qualities that are needed to reach your goals easier and faster.

The Mind-Changing Habit of Journaling

Understand where your negative self-image, bad habits, and unhealthy thoughts come from. Know yourself to change yourself. Embrace the life-changing transformation potential of journaling. This book shows you how to use the ultimate self-healing tool of journaling to find your own answers to your most pressing problems, discover your true self and lead a life of growth mindset.

The Unlimited Mind

This book collects all the tips, tricks and tactics of the most successful people to develop your inner smartness.

The Unlimited Mind will show you how to think smarter and find your inner genius. This book is a collection of research and scientific studies about better decision-making, fairer judgments, and intuition improvement. It takes a critical look at our everyday cognitive habits and points out small but serious mistakes that are easily correctable.

Unshakable Resilience

How do you keep going when things fall apart? How do you find purpose and meaning in uncertainty?

Build a resilient mindset immune to adversity. We all face common pain, difficulty, and insecurity. We live in an unpredictable environment we cannot control. The only way out of it is through it. Strengthening our resilience muscle and awakening the warrior in each of us has never been more important. This book offers practical tools to take back control of our lives.

Who You Were Meant To Be

Discover the strengths of your personality and how to use them to make better life choices. In Who You Were Born To Be, you'll learn some of the most influential personality-related studies. Thanks to these studies you'll learn to capitalize on your strengths, and how you can you become the best version of yourself.

Wired For Confidence

Do you feel like you just aren't good enough? End this vicious thought cycle NOW. Wired For Confidence tells you the necessary steps to break out from the pits of low self-esteem, lowered expectations, and lack of assertiveness. Take the first step to creating the life you only dared to dream of.

To access the full list of my books visit this link.

References:

Changing Minds. Projection. Changing Minds. 2020. http://changingminds.org/explanations/behaviors/coping/projection.htm

Chodron, Pema. When Things Fall Apart. Sambhala. 2000.

Legg. Timothy J. PhD. Everything You Need to Know About Anxiety. Healthline. 2018.
https://www.healthline.com/health/anxiety-symptoms

Mayo Clinic Staff. Denial. Mayo Clinic. 2020. https://www.mayoclinic.org/healthy-lifestyle/adult-health/in-depth/denial/art-20047926

McLeod, Saul. Defense Mechanisms. Simply Psychology. 2019. https://www.simplypsychology.org/defense-mechanisms.html

Paul, Sherly. The Wisdom of Anxiety. Sounds True. 2019.

Premier Health. Beware High Levels of Cortisol, the Stress Hormone. Premier Health. 2017. https://www.premierhealth.com/your-health/articles/women-wisdom-wellness-/beware-high-levels-of-cortisol-the-stress-hormone

Psychology Today. Defense Mechanisms. Psychology Today. 2020. https://www.psychologytoday.com/us/basics/defense-mechanisms

Reitan, Ann. Dissociation and Psychosis. Brain Blogger. 2015. http://www.brainblogger.com/2015/05/21/dissociation-and-psychosis/

Rethink Mental Disorder. Dissociation and dissociative identity disorder (DID). Rethink Mental Disorder. 2020. https://www.rethink.org/advice-and-information/about-mental-illness/learn-more-about-conditions/dissociation-and-dissociative-identity-disorder-did/

Endnotes

[i] Paul, Sherly. The Wisdom of Anxiety. Sounds True. 2019.
[ii] Legg. Timothy J. PhD. Everything You Need to Know About Anxiety. Healthline. 2018.
https://www.healthline.com/health/anxiety-symptoms
[iii] Chodron, Pema. When Things Fall Apart. Sambhala. 2000.
[iv] McLeod, Saul. Defense Mechanisms. Simply Psychology. 2019.
https://www.simplypsychology.org/defense-mechanisms.html
[v] Reitan, Ann. Dissociation and Psychosis. Brain Blogger. 2015.
http://www.brainblogger.com/2015/05/21/dissociation-and-psychosis/
[vi] Rethink Mental Disorder. Dissociation and dissociative identity disorder (DID).

Rethink Mental Disorder. 2020. https://www.rethink.org/advice-and-information/about-mental-illness/learn-more-about-conditions/dissociation-and-dissociative-identity-disorder-did/

[vii] Premier Health. Beware High Levels of Cortisol, the Stress Hormone. Premier Health. 2017. https://www.premierhealth.com/your-health/articles/women-wisdom-wellness-/beware-high-levels-of-cortisol-the-stress-hormone

[viii] Psychology Today. Defense Mechanisms. Psychology Today. 2020. https://www.psychologytoday.com/us/basics/defense-mechanisms

[ix] Mayo Clinic Staff. Denial. Mayo Clinic. 2020. https://www.mayoclinic.org/healthy-lifestyle/adult-health/in-depth/denial/art-20047926

[x] Changing Minds. Projection. Changing Minds. 2020. http://changingminds.org/explanations/behaviors/coping/projection.htm

[xi] McLeod, Saul. Defense Mechanisms. Simply Psychology. 2019. https://www.simplypsychology.org/defense-mechanisms.html

www.ingramcontent.com/pod-product-compliance
Lightning Source LLC
Chambersburg PA
CBHW020107240426
43661CB00002B/58